100

THINGS TO DO IN
JACKSONVILLE
BEFORE YOU
DIE

100

THINGS TO DO IN
JACKSONVILLE
BEFORE YOU
DIE

• •

AMY WEST

Library of Congress Control Number: 2020937358

ISBN: 9781681062709

Design by Jill Halpin

Printed in the United States of America
20 21 22 23 24   5 4 3 2 1

We (the publisher and the author) have done our best to provide the most accurate
information available when this book was completed. However, we make no
warranty, guaranty or promise about the accuracy, completeness or currency of the
information provided, and we expressly disclaim all warranties, express or implied.
Please note that attractions, company names, addresses, websites, and phone
numbers are subject to change or closure, and this is outside of our control. We are
not responsible for any loss, damage, injury, or inconvenience that may occur due
to the use of this book. When exploring new destinations, please do your homework
before you go. You are responsible for your own safety and health when using this
book.

DEDICATION

To my mom, Stephanie, for being brave enough to pack up your little girl and head for the promised land.

CONTENTS

Preface. xiii

Acknowledgments. xv

Food and Drink

1. Wine and Dine at Eleven South Bistro & Bar 2

2. Get a Taste of Naples at V Pizza 3

3. Let Them Eat Cake at Biscottis 4

4. Sip On a Cup of Joe at Bold Bean Coffee Roasters 5

5. Enjoy Sunday Brunch at Vernon's 6

6. Get Your Fill of Pumpkin Spice at Cinotti's Bakery and
   Sandwich Shop. 7

7. Nibble on Gator Tail at Clark's Fish Camp 8

8. Take a Dip at Dreamette 9

9. Chat with the Chef at Restaurant Doro 10

10. Enjoy the Bird's-Eye View at River and Post's Rooftop Lounge . . . 12

11. Go Tiki at Flask and Cannon. 13

12. Join the Sandwich Crew at the French Pantry 14

13. Drink Your Trail Off on the Jacksonville Ale Trail 16

14. Feel the Island Vibes at Lemon Bar. 17

15. Get in the Spirit at Manifest Distillery. 18

16. Cover It in Peruvian Sauce at Angie's Subs. 19

17. Gourmet Your Patty at M Shack 20

18. Think Small at Mini Bar Donuts 21

19. Enjoy a Taste of France at Orsay 22

20. Taste the First Coast at Safe Harbor Seafood Restaurant. 23

21. Reserve a Seat at Salt's Kitchen Table. 24

22. Embrace the Harvest at Congaree and Penn 26

23. Celebrate in Style at Cowford Chophouse 27

24. Fiesta at TacoLu. 28

25. Join the Neighborhood Crowd while Dining at Taverna 29

26. Find Your Vintage at Royal Palms Village Wine & Tapas 30

27. Become a Regular at Maple Street Biscuit Company 32

28. Get Together at Town Hall. 33

29. Put a Little South in Your Mouth at Bearded Pig 34

Music and Entertainment

30. Celebrate Your Independence during 4th of July in Jax Beach 38

31. Look to the Skies at the Sea and Sky Air Show 40

32. Enjoy Dinner and a Show at Alhambra Theatre and Dining 41

33. Demand an Encore at the Veterans Memorial Arena. 42

34. Chill Out at the Jacksonville Jazz Festival. 43

• •

35. Get Footloose at Dancin' in the Streets 44

36. Tailgate before the Florida-Georgia Game 45

37. Listen Up at the Blue Jay Listening Room 46

38. Laugh Out Loud at the Florida Theatre 48

39. Start Thanksgiving at Pete's Bar 49

40. Jam On at Porchfest 50

41. Watch a Silver Screen Classic at San Marco Theatre 51

42. Listen to Blues on the Beach at Springing the Blues. 52

43. Screen an Indie at Sun-Ray Cinema 53

44. Volunteer at Theatre Jacksonville 54

45. Traverse the Globe at the World of Nations Celebration 55

46. Watch the Showdown Unfold at Fish to Fork 56

47. Become a Sandcastle Artisan at Opening of the Beaches 57

48. Go behind the Scenes at Sally Dark Rides. 58

Sports and Recreation

49. Make a Splash at Adventure Landing 62

50. Thrill to an Airboat Adventure with Sea Serpent Tours 63

51. Find Renewal in Nature at Jacksonville Arboretum & Gardens 64

52. Bike the Baldwin Rail Trail. 66

53. Play like a Champion at THE PLAYERS Stadium Course 67

54. Hunt for Sharks' Teeth at Guana Reserve's Middle Beach 68

• •

55. Go Camping at Kathryn Abbey Hanna Park 69

56. Drive on the Beach at Huguenot Memorial Park. 70

57. Get Horsey at the Jacksonville Equestrian Center 72

58. Beat Feet at the Gate River Run. 73

59. Explore Skeleton Beach. 74

60. Support Du-u-u-uval at a Jacksonville Jaguars Game 75

61. Finish the Donna 76

62. Have Good Old-Fashioned Fun with the
Jacksonville Jumbo Shrimp 78

63. Catch the Big One off Jacksonville Beach Fishing Pier. 79

64. Attend THE PLAYERS Championship. 80

65. Take a Cruise with the St. Johns River Taxi and Tours. 82

66. Have a Spa Day at the Ritz-Carlton 83

67. Stand-Up Paddleboard at Jax Surf and Paddle. 84

Culture and History

68. Walk through History at the Beaches Museum 88

69. Order Tapas on the Rooftop at the Casa Marina Hotel 90

70. Admire the Luxury at *Concours d'Elegance* 91

71. Attend a Night Feeding at Catty Shack Ranch. 92

72. Catch an Open House at CoRK Art District 94

73. Take a Hike at Fort Caroline National Memorial 95

74. Do Your Research at the Jacksonville Library Main Branch. 96

● ●

75. Cross the River on the St. Johns River Ferry 97

76. Take a Walk on the Wild Side at the Jacksonville
Zoo and Gardens 98

77. Learn from the Past at the Kingsley Plantation 100

78. Traverse the Currents of Time at the Museum
of Science and History 101

79. Tune In to the Jacksonville Symphony 102

80. Celebrate African American Heritage at the
Ritz Theatre and Museum 104

81. Picnic under Treaty Oak 105

82. Watch a Historical Reenactment at Fort Clinch State Park 106

83. Peruse the Art of Our Time at the MOCA 107

84. Cruise through the Brumos Collection 108

85. Meander through the Gardens at Cummer Museum
of Art and Gardens 109

86. Take a Selfie Tour of the Jacksonville Murals 110

Shopping and Fashion

87. Shop with the Cool Kids in Five Points 114

88. Support Local Artists at Art Walk 115

89. Collect Your Next Art Piece at Atlantic Beach Arts Market 116

90. Enjoy the Beach Life at Beaches Town Center 117

91. Lose Yourself in Chamblin Bookmine 118

92. Wander through San Marco 119

93. Go Treasure Hunting at Riverside Arts Market 120

94. Update Your Look at Sawgrass Markets 122

95. Transform Old to New at Eco Relics 123

96. Fall in Love with Historic Fernandina Beach 124

97. Walk and Shop at the Shoppes of Avondale 125

98. Satisfy Your Sweet Tooth at Sweet Pete's Candy 126

99. Make Time for Tea at Ashes Boutique and Tea Room 128

100. Get Your Retail Therapy at St. Johns Town Center 130

Suggested Itineraries 133

Activities by Season 137

Index 139

PREFACE

How do you define Jacksonville? Well, it's complicated. As the largest city in the continental US, it has a universe of micro-cultures one could spend years getting familiar with. Originally known as Cowford for the passage on the St. Johns River where cattle herders used to ford their livestock, today you might hear the city referred to as the First Coast, the Bold New City of the South, or simply Jax.

The history of this region is diverse and directly tied to the bodies of water in and around it. Over the centuries, the Atlantic Ocean, St. Johns River, and Intracoastal Waterway have offered industry, sustenance, and strategic defense positions for those who called it home. Situated on the Northeast shore of the Florida peninsula, Jacksonville enjoys nearly year-round sunny weather, and attracts residents who enjoy the outdoor lifestyle.

Jacksonville can boast the state's largest urban park system, a dynamic art scene, its own NFL team, and an impressive lineup of culinary gems. Folks here are generally friendly and laid back with a Southern sense of hospitality. Many of the residents of the city are transplants who've relocated to Jax for its reasonable cost of living, warm weather, and opportunities in a variety of fields such as medicine, military, and finance.

It's my hope that this book sparks in you a sense of

• •

adventure and encourages you to get out there and explore this great city. Whether you're a lifer, a new resident, or a first-time visitor, Jacksonville (and I) welcome you to embrace its warmth and hospitality. Get outdoors, see a game, go back in time, and discover your next dining destination right here on the First Coast.

—Amy West

ACKNOWLEDGMENTS

Although many hours are spent writing in solitude, no book can be written entirely alone, especially one that involves in-depth knowledge of such a diverse city. It has been my privilege to get to know Jacksonville as a resident over the last 30 years. I am inspired by its evolution and the warmth of the people who make up this community. I've had the most fun rediscovering my city as a writer over the last decade. It is with gratitude that I acknowledge these important figures who've been so generous with their insights.

Thank you to my husband David: my partner in crime, fellow adventurer, and avid supporter of my creative side for over 15 years. Without your unconditional love and tolerance for all my zany ideas, I could not have traveled the road I'm on now. You are where my home is. You have been my fellow traveler, photographer, and reviewer all these years. Your opinions have always been valued, and our different points of view find balance together.

Thank you, also, to our two girls, Sienna and London, who patiently waited on Mom during hours of research, drafting, editing, revisions, and events. I hope this book inspires you to set out on your own adventures, beginning in your own backyard.

Thank you to Reedy Press for believing in my insight and offering me this opportunity to shine a spotlight on this city I believe in so much.

Thank you to my best friend Sophia, who modeled what it means to be a new author in this modern social landscape and who has cheered me on the whole way. Your insight and wisdom have been invaluable, and there's no other mom I'd choose to go into battle with. We are opposite sides of the same coin, and whatever world we live in, I'll always find you. Thank you for always having my six.

To Grant Smith, thank you for your professional insight and wealth of advice and feedback. I appreciate your expertise. To Patty Winter and the entire team at Visit Jacksonville, thank you for developing a relationship with this burgeoning travel writer almost a decade ago. Your faith in my words and willingness to lend a helping hand have always been valued. Special thanks to the restaurateurs, small business owners, PR professionals, and community advocates who have opened up your places of business to me over the years. It is my hope that your hospitality and investment in the writers, media, and influencers of this city will be returned tenfold.

Finally, I want to thank my friends, family, and followers who have encouraged me along my journey. Your likes, comments, feedback, and engagement have kept me motivated and have influenced my work along the way.

Photo courtesy of Kristen Penoyer

Photo courtesy of Amy West

FOOD AND DRINK

WINE AND DINE
AT ELEVEN SOUTH BISTRO & BAR

Eleven South never ceases to delight and surprise with their innovative scratch menu and timeless selection of wine. Erroneously thought of as a date-night destination only, Eleven South has something for all diners, budgets, and hours. With 15 consecutive *Wine Spectator* Awards of Excellence and counting, a visit to Eleven South is a must in Jacksonville Beach. Inspired by fine dining throughout the Mediterranean and Europe, each dish is conceived as a pairing with a wine profile. The Premium Happy Hour is the perfect place to get acquainted with all the culinary treasures at Eleven South. Cozy up to the bar, get to know the talented wait staff, and enjoy the delicate vintage the bartender pairs with each tasty treat such as Truffled Parmesan Frites or Old School Steak Sliders.

216 11th Ave. South, Jacksonville Beach, FL 32250
(904) 241-1112
www.elevensouth.com

TIP
Lunch is also a great time to experience Eleven South's seasonal scratch menu and promises not to break the bank.

GET A TASTE OF NAPLES
AT V PIZZA

True Neapolitan pizza is hard to come by, but thanks to three locals, you can now find it in Jacksonville. Cultivated with the finest ingredients, the menu at V Pizza would make any Italian proud. Imported from the old country, you'll find San Marzano tomatoes, *mozzarella di bufala*, 00 flour, and *prosciutto di Parma* on the line-up of authentic ingredients from the most iconic regions in Italy. Authenticity is key, and V's quality standards are high, so order a drink and grab a slice of Naples' finest, prepared fresh right here in Jacksonville.

528 1st St. North, Jacksonville Beach, FL 32250
(904) 853-6633
www.vpizza.com

LET THEM EAT CAKE
AT BISCOTTIS

Your experience in Jacksonville isn't complete without a visit to the historic neighborhood of Avondale. Anchoring this charming residential borough is a string of shops and restaurants. One of the most beloved spots in the Shoppes of Avondale is Biscottis restaurant. For over 25 years, Biscottis has been a go-to culinary staple for foodies and friends. Known for its eclectic fine-dining menu and scratch kitchen, Biscotti's is perhaps most famous for its dessert case. Delicate pastries, indulgent creme brûlée, and one of the most iconic selections of cake in the region all create a valid excuse to grab an espresso and order dessert first!

3556 St. Johns Ave.
(904) 387-2060
biscottis.net

SIP ON A CUP OF JOE
AT BOLD BEAN COFFEE ROASTERS

If you're looking for the perfect cup of craft coffee in the "Bold New City of the South," look no further than Jacksonville's own Bold Bean Coffee. Partnering with over 30 local businesses, chances are you'll have a cup of Bold Bean sooner rather than later. For the most authentic experience, head to one of their several locations around town, which include Riverside, the Beaches, and San Marco. Each locale thrives on the culture of its individual neighborhood, and—true to Bold Bean's Mission—you'll find community, a good time, and outstanding coffee.

869 Stockton St.
(904) 853-6545
boldbeancoffee.com

TIP
Don't forget to purchase a bag to grind and brew at home. There's nothing more "Jacksonville" than waking up to Bold Bean's fresh roasted blends.

ENJOY SUNDAY BRUNCH
AT VERNON'S

When it comes to being the "best in brunch," competition can be fierce on the First Coast. However, Vernon's First Coast Kitchen and Bar makes standing out seem effortless. Housed in the renowned Sawgrass Marriott Golf Resort and Spa, this signature restaurant's brunch has more to offer than the average morning lineup. Every Sunday, the culinary team orchestrates its brunch service around a unique theme. They delight in surprising and tantalizing your senses from the fresh catch to the omelet station, even including a special brunch bar just for kids (with a craft table). As an avid supporter of the local community, Vernon's chefs craft tasty dishes from the freshest local ingredients, including some from the resort's own garden. Enjoy live music while you brunch, and let the kids be entertained in the interactive kids' corner, ensuring that you do what Sundays do best—relax and enjoy good company and great food.

1000 PGA Tour Blvd., Ponte Vedra Beach, FL 32082
(904) 285-7777
www.marriott.com/hotels/travel/
jaxsw-sawgrass-marriott-golf-resort-and-spa/

GET YOUR FILL OF PUMPKIN SPICE
AT CINOTTI'S BAKERY AND SANDWICH SHOP

Neighborhood bakeries are the framework of childhood memories. Colorful confections tempt your palate, and the haze of flour and sugar left behind create a cloud of sweetness you can physically taste. Cinotti's is no exception to this rule and has been the anchor of family and neighborhood traditions for generations. Whether you stop in for morning donuts or a deli sandwich for lunch, you are bound to run into a familiar face. Indeed, there's something about this family-run destination that invites you to make yourself at home. Known for their holiday specialties such as pumpkin pie, Thanksgiving dinner, and their cult-favorite pumpkin spice donuts, Cinotti's is the place you can count on to make every occasion special. You don't have to wait around for a holiday to make an appearance, though. Any day is a great day to stop by and enjoy one of their masterful sweet creations. Just don't forget the coffee!

1523 Penman Rd., Jacksonville Beach, FL 32250
(904) 246-1728
cinottisbakery.com/

NIBBLE ON GATOR TAIL
AT CLARK'S FISH CAMP

Home of one of the largest privately owned taxidermy collections in the country, Clark's Fish Camp is a legendary dining destination in Jacksonville. Guests come to marvel at the motionless menagerie that includes tigers, monkeys, giraffes, bears, gators, and deer while experiencing waterfront dining on Julington Creek. Clark's menu takes a walk on the wild side for adventurous carnivores that include gator, shark, yak, and camel. More conservative tastebuds will recognize and enjoy coastal-inspired crowd-pleasers like *ahi* tuna, shrimp, and seasonal fresh catch. Seafood platters, signature cocktails, and an extensive raw bar round out your choices with plenty of options to please your entire table. Clark's Fish Camp is an experience worth going out of your way for. By water or land, make your way to this unique dining destination on the First Coast for a meal you're not likely to forget.

12903 Hood Landing Rd.
(904) 268-3474
clarksfishcamp.net

TAKE A DIP
AT DREAMETTE

As the saying goes, "Nothing beats the original." Locals agree that soft-serve ice cream in Jacksonville doesn't get more original than Dreamette. Dishing out soft serve since 1948, Dreamette has achieved icon status in the Bold City—so much so that it's not unusual to stand in line for a bit while eagerly waiting to satisfy your sweet tooth. Priding themselves on the quality of their product, Dreamette's staff serves authentic soft serve with top-quality ingredients. Known for their dipped cones, hand-spun milkshakes, and over-the-top sundaes, the staff makes sure to serve them up with a generous hand. For decades, this Murray Hill staple has pleased generations of guests, and it's not uncommon to find those same kids who grew up on their cones returning with their young families for those chocolate, peanut butter, or cake batter-dipped cones.

3646 Post St.
(904) 388-2558
m.facebook.com/Dreamette

TIP
Dreamette is cash only, so make sure to hit the ATM before you visit.

CHAT WITH THE CHEF
AT RESTAURANT DORO

The First Coast offers masters of the culinary trade plenty of locally sourced ingredients for crafting a delicious meal. Nowhere do these ingredients come to life quite like they do at Restaurant Doro. Owner/Executive Chef Chris Polidoro brought his extensive experience in fine dining with him when he relocated from New York to Neptune Beach. He's been inspiring taste buds ever since in his elegantly appointed space that feels both fresh and delightfully private with a modern coastal aesthetic. A meal at Doro makes you feel both comfortably at home and like you're experiencing true artistry come together in front of you. Each bite seems to burst with flavor, largely due to the great intention Polidoro uses to source the ingredients, including the finest organic produce and humanely raised meat with seasonal features and menu favorites like grilled snapper and crispy short ribs. Innovation meets charm and relaxed coastal vibes when you find a seat at Restaurant Doro.

106 First St., Neptune Beach, FL 32266
(904) 853-6943
restaurantdoro.com

TIP

Make an effort to score a seat at the bar to watch
Chef Chris work his craft and perhaps share a story
or two about his travels while you imbibe on a
perfectly paired vintage.

ENJOY THE BIRD'S-EYE VIEW
AT RIVER AND POST'S ROOFTOP LOUNGE

Jacksonville is blessed with a bounty of waterfront views. From the Atlantic Ocean to the St. Johns River, our residents don't have to look far to enjoy the scenery. The best perspective is likely to be the bird's-eye view, one that River and Post captured with their chic Rooftop Lounge. Handcrafted cocktails, such as the Great Fire (a nod to the great fire that destroyed Jacksonville) that features jalapeno-infused tequila, pair elegantly with the sweeping skyline of downtown Jacksonville and the St. Johns River. Firepits add ambiance and warmth to chilly nights, and the glow of neon strikes a mood for dining and date nights. Order some charcuterie, toast to good times, and watch the sunset over the Bold City at River and Post.

1000 Riverside Ave. #100
(904) 575-2366
www.riverandpostjax.com/

GO TIKI
AT FLASK AND CANNON

The beaches of Jacksonville have more than a few hip watering holes to brag about, but only one has pulled together a menu featuring over 100 rums from around the globe. Retro-styled with a little bit of South Pacific influence that spans from Hawaii to Havana, Flask and Cannon has carved out a niche for itself that puts it in a class all its own in Jax. You won't find just rum on the menu—whatever you drink flies! Beer, wine, and all the spirits in between make Flask and Cannon a bar worth visiting for all. Situated just steps from the beach, this modern tiki joint is a place where you can enjoy live music, trivia, and sports TV. And if you've got an appetite from spending hours in the Florida sunshine, you're in luck because V Pizza operates synergistically with Flask and Cannon, which allows you to order from either menu. So, grab a slice and tiki up; you're about to have a fun night!

528 1st St. North, Jacksonville Beach, FL 32250
(904) 853-6633
flaskandcannon.com

JOIN THE SANDWICH CREW
AT THE FRENCH PANTRY

Few businesses make the leap in status from cult following to legendary, but French Pantry has managed to do just that. When the original owners relocated from California to Jacksonville, they set out to capitalize on lessons learned from rubbing shoulders with masters in the cooking craft such as Wolfgang Puck. That experience came together when they launched a commercial bakery. Demands from teenagers at a nearby high school inspired them to offer a selection of sandwiches. With time, that original sandwich crew turned into the cult following French Pantry enjoys today. Among menu favorites are an extensive variety of bruschettas; warm, cold, and pressed sandwiches; and generous salads crafted with the freshest ingredients. Although servings are healthy, guests should always be sure to leave room for one of the decadent desserts French Pantry makes from scratch. The ambiance is casual with a focus on what's most important: food and friends. Pull up a chair, and make sure to leave room for dessert!

6301 Powers Ave.
(904) 730-8696
thefrenchpantry.com/

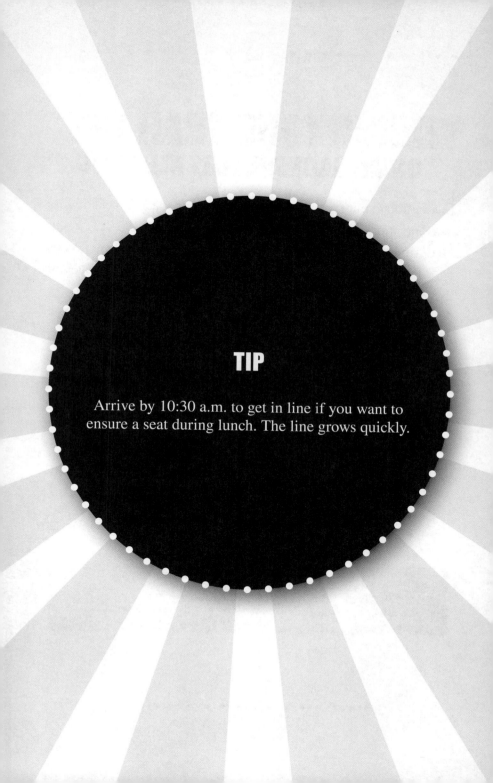

TIP

Arrive by 10:30 a.m. to get in line if you want to
ensure a seat during lunch. The line grows quickly.

DRINK YOUR TRAIL OFF
ON THE JACKSONVILLE ALE TRAIL

In addition to our river, beaches, and outdoor spaces, Jacksonville has one more trail to boast about: the Jacksonville Ale Trail. Featuring the Bold City's top craft breweries, the Ale Trail invites beer lovers far and wide to explore the city through the eyes of its best brews. Visitors need only to pick up a passport at one of the affiliated breweries to begin. The more locations you check off your list, the more swag you can earn. Over 20 destinations are listed on the trail, including Intuition Ale Works in downtown Jacksonville, Wicked Barley Brewing in Jacksonville's Southside, and Green Room Brewing at the Beaches. Partner up with a friend, and (as they say) drink your trail off!

208 N. Laura St., Ste. 102
(800) 733-2668
www.visitjacksonville.com/jax-ale-trail

TIP
Drink responsibly and take advantage of great guided tours that are offered around Jax like the Jax Brew Bus or Go Tuk'n brewery tours.

FEEL THE ISLAND VIBES
AT LEMON BAR

Voted the number one beach bar in Jax and beyond, the Lemon Bar is a beachside essential. Located in charming Neptune Beach, Lemon Bar is the perfect place to kick back and order a margarita while you soak up the sun on the oceanfront patio and nosh on classics like grilled cheese, tacos, and hot dogs. Loved by locals and visitors alike, it's easy to find a seat and run into old friends or make new ones when you're surrounded by all the island vibes Lemon puts out. It's hard not to feel good in the presence of the ocean breeze, sea-salt air, comfort food, and tropical drinks. Daily specials, live music, and a kickin' happy hour are a few of the many reasons to go out of your way for a visit to Lemon Bar.

2 Lemon St., Neptune Beach, FL 32266
(904) 372-0487
www.lemonbarjax.com

TIP

Make sure to bring your ID. You must be 21 or older to imbibe at Lemon; they card everyone.

GET IN THE SPIRIT
AT MANIFEST DISTILLERY

In addition to its growing craft brew scene, Jacksonville has a full-scale organic distillery located right in the heart of downtown's Sports District. Within its lineup, you'll find organic rye whiskey, organic gin, and non-GMO potato vodka. Manifest even shows off its hometown spirit with a Florida citrus vodka. The distillery was founded with a commitment to American craftsmanship, and it shows. From its American-made equipment to a partnership with North American co-ops to source the distillery's grain, Manifest's products are crafted after the highest form of spirit making. Visitors are invited to schedule a tour, available by appointment, and experience the passion and care that goes into every bottle. At the end of your tour, samples are provided, so you can taste the quality Manifest has to offer for yourself.

960 E. Forsyth St.
(904) 619-1479
www.manifestdistilling.com

COVER IT IN PERUVIAN SAUCE
AT ANGIE'S SUBS

When hunger strikes and you find yourself in Jacksonville Beach, go where the locals go. Home of the famous Peruvian Sub, Angie's following rivals that of any sub shop in town. Located in a renovated convenience store, Angie's has since expanded into the laundromat next door and boasts a haphazard "yard sale" vibe. One could argue that it's precisely what makes this hip sub shop such a scene. Everyone has their favorite order at Angie's, but one thing is almost universally true: any sub you order is best served drenched in Peruvian sauce. Order some tea, add some sauce to your sub, and ask for it "crunchy" (they'll add twisty BBQ Fritos) for a true Jax Beach meal.

1436 Beach Blvd., Jacksonville Beach, FL 32250
(904) 246-2519
www.facebook.com/angiessubs

TIP
Call ahead for the fastest service.

GOURMET YOUR PATTY
AT M SHACK

The Medure brothers are widely known in Jax for their fine-dining restaurants Matthew's and Medure, but perhaps the most trafficked of their concepts is M Shack. Offering crafted gourmet burgers from fresh-ground, hormone-free beef in addition to hand-cut fries, juicy beef hot dogs, and the ever-popular kale salad, M Shack has cultivated a truly thoughtful menu for the modern diner. Hankering for something sweet? Don't leave the Shack without one of their flavorful milkshakes served up virgin or—depending on location—spiked.

10281 Mid Town Parkway
(904) 642-5000
www.mshackburgers.com

THINK SMALL
AT MINI BAR DONUTS

It's not every day you can eat four donuts with little-to-no guilt, but at Mini Bar Donuts, that's not so extraordinary. Coming in at a third of the average-sized donut, Mini Bar's made-to-order donuts are delivered hot and fresh in 19 signature flavors. Mini Bar not only successfully taps into deep-rooted childhood memories with flavors like Pop-Tart, Samoa, and Fruity Pebbles, but they also make it their mission to partner with as many local businesses as possible. On weekends, Mini Bar serves up special flavors for the donut aficionado, and their social media-savvy fans scramble to be the first to find out what flavor will be featured. Mini Bar has a major local following, and it's easy to see why this family-friendly business is such a success.

1300 Beach Blvd., Jacksonville Beach, FL 32250
(904) 372-4765
minibardonuts.com

ENJOY A TASTE OF FRANCE
AT ORSAY

Jacksonville's Southern coastal geography comes with a lifestyle that's noticeably more laid back than that of the average metropolitan city. Drawing fine diners from all over Jacksonville and beyond to its quiet location in historic Avondale, Orsay offers unpretentious elegance and sophisticated fare paired with notable Southern influences. Whether you're dining on brunch al fresco, sipping craft cocktails at the bar, celebrating an anniversary in the formal dining area, or relaxing in the rustic dining room for a meal with friends, you're sure to be impressed with a menu selection everyone can enjoy. Each dish includes ingredients responsibly sourced from local and regional purveyors. From the raw bar and the Maple Leaf Duck to the elegant French macarons, you'll feel transported to France while getting a distinct taste of Jax when you dine at award-winning Orsay.

3630 Park St.
(904) 381-0909
restaurantorsay.com

TASTE THE FIRST COAST
AT SAFE HARBOR
SEAFOOD RESTAURANT

If you're looking for an authentic taste of the First Coast, it won't get fresher than at Safe Harbor Seafood Restaurant. Each morning, Safe Harbor scoops up the day's catch from Mayport shrimp boats and brings it directly to hungry guests. Safe Harbor's flagship location is situated right in the middle of Mayport's historic shrimping grounds. Relax in the laid-back atmosphere, and enjoy views of the St. Johns River while you dine inside or al fresco. Fan favorites on the menu include generous portions of wild-caught shrimp, blackened scallops, the fried-fish sandwich, and fresh-caught oysters. Choose your seafood catch, and they'll make it to your specifications. Not at all pretentious, this is a come-as-you-are seafood shack focused on fresh food and an authentic atmosphere.

4378 Ocean St., Mayport, FL 32233
(904) 246-4911
www.safeharborseafoodrestaurant.com

TIP
It's not uncommon to find a long line on the weekends. Show up before noon for the quickest service.

RESERVE A SEAT
AT SALT'S KITCHEN TABLE

Ask any chef what the most important ingredient in their kitchen is, and you'll likely hear the same answer: salt. AAA Five Diamond restaurant Salt is widely accepted as the epitome of fine dining in the Jacksonville region. Reserve a seat at the famed Kitchen Table for a culinary experience that will delight and inspire. Up to four guests can dine at the Table, which is only seated once a night. You'll get up close and personal with an interactive look at the preparation for the evening's meal as the culinary team presents a multicourse masterpiece for your enjoyment created by the chef specifically for you. Each dish is elegantly paired with a wine that will highlight and enhance the flavor profile of each simple yet elevated ingredient. Salt's menu includes the freshest ingredients from land and sea executed in a simple yet intentional way with an eye for creative and interactive plating such as a smoke-filled cloche for smoked prawns and salt blocks heated up to high temps to finish your tenderloin at the table. Dinner at Salt's Kitchen Table is an adventure for your taste buds that will connect you to the region via the senses. Come hungry, and enjoy a showcase of fine culinary achievement whose reputation speaks for itself.

The Ritz-Carlton, Amelia Island
4750 Amelia Island Parkway, Amelia Island, FL 32034
(904) 277-1100
www.ritzcarlton.com/en/hotels/florida/amelia-island/dining/salt

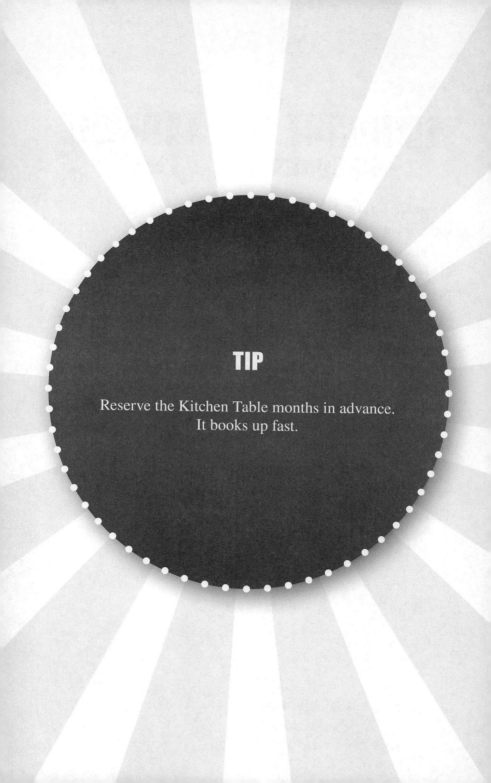

TIP

Reserve the Kitchen Table months in advance.
It books up fast.

EMBRACE THE HARVEST
AT CONGAREE AND PENN

It might surprise you to learn that the Florida climate is ideal for growing rice. With our high humidity and clay-rich soil, the moisture creates a fine environment for the rice to develop. Originally established in 2014 as a fish farm, Congaree and Penn received such great feedback on a side crop of rice that they quickly changed course. Since then has grown to include diverse offerings, including the largest orchard of mayhaw trees in the world. Congaree also houses "you-pick" vines, fancy chickens, and thousands of honey-producing bees. Here on the farm, Congaree welcomes guests to learn and grow together, embracing all things in the collective spirits of agriculture, culinary art, and community. Take a sunset "cruise" across the farm's 350 acres on a tractor-pulled wagon, hike the farm with a friendly goat, or dine in style on locally grown fare as you relax and connect with nature.

11830 Old Kings Rd.
(904) 527-1945
www.congareeandpenn.com

CELEBRATE IN STYLE
AT COWFORD CHOPHOUSE

Housed in a cherished city landmark you'll find one of the city's most prestigious steak houses: Cowford Chophouse. The restaurant was a passion project of restaurateur Jacques Klempf, who dreamt of bringing a piece of Bold City's history back to life. Lovingly restored and redesigned to capture the romance of times gone by, Cowford is the steakhouse you can count on to impress any guest. Whether you're here for rooftop cocktails overlooking the St. Johns River at sunset, dining out for that special occasion, or sealing a paramount business deal, Cowford is a setting that won't disappoint. Satiate your appetite with fresh catch or premium cuts of beef and savory *à la carte* sides while being delighted by exceptional service. There's always a sense of sophistication and style, and it's the ideal location for dining before or after the big game or sold-out concert.

101 E. Bay St.
(904) 862-6464
cowfordchophouse.com

TIP
Prepare to tip a valet for the easiest parking option.

FIESTA
AT TACOLU

There has been much debate over the "Signature Jacksonville Dish." Although the discussion rages on, a strong contender for that coveted title is the fish taco. Serving up one of the city's most sought-after fish tacos is none other than TacoLu, a locally established mom-and-pop, Baja street taco shop with a huge following. Dishing out tasty handhelds, TacoLu overcame great odds to establish itself during the recession of 2008. Over the years, this beloved Jax Beach icon—named for the owners' daughter Lucy—has outgrown its original location and has taken up residence in the historic Homestead restaurant space. It's here you'll find an extensive menu of tequilas that keeps aficionados and newbies coming back for more while the festive atmosphere proves why life at the beaches is so dang cool.

1712 Beach Blvd., Jacksonville Beach, FL 32250
(904) 249-8226
www.tacolu.com

TIP
TacoLu is closed on Monday; plan accordingly.

JOIN THE NEIGHBORHOOD CROWD
WHILE DINING AT TAVERNA

Established by Chef/Wine director team and married couple Sam and Kiley Efron, Taverna is set apart by its rustic atmosphere and modern take on fresh Italian cuisine. Combining their world-class training and experience, the two became a powerful pair on the culinary scene of Jax and have racked up several awards. An impressive wine list combines with a creative cocktail menu, all pairing exquisitely with crowd favorites like herbed ricotta, wood-fired pizzas, and house-made pasta. Don't miss great value from Taverna's happy hour menu Monday through Friday, and be sure to add this destination to your weekend brunch plans for the crepes, breakfast pizzas, and elegant pastries.

1986 San Marco Blvd.
(904) 398-3005
taverna.restaurant

TIP
Taverna offers a variety of vegan and gluten-free options. Feel free to make special requests for guests with dietary restrictions.

FIND YOUR VINTAGE
AT ROYAL PALMS
VILLAGE WINE & TAPAS

Walking into Royal Palms Village Wine & Tapas feels a bit like you've been transported to a tasting room in wine country. Equal parts retail and restaurant, Royal Palms is unique to Jacksonville and offers diners the ability to choose a vintage right off the shelf and enjoy it during their meal or take it home to sip and savor at their leisure. With over 1,200 bottles of fine wine and 200 bottles of craft beer, you won't have any problems finding the perfect pairing for Royal's tasty tapas. Fresh farm-to-table ingredients make up the modern menu based on inspiration garnered from Spain to California. Dine inside or feast al fresco on the patio surrounded by their organic edible garden. It's always festive at Royal Palms, and if you come on the right night, you'll enjoy live music or a wine tasting. It's an eclectic destination celebrating art, good food, fine wine, and craft brew, and you can be sure it's always a good time.

296 Royal Palms Dr., Atlantic Beach, FL 32233
(904) 372-0052
www.royalpalmwines.com

TIP

On Mondays, Royal Palms features free corkage. Select a bottle, and savor your wine choice at the retail price as you dine. No markup!

BECOME A REGULAR
AT MAPLE STREET BISCUIT COMPANY

Known for their signature buttermilk biscuits, Maple Street recrafts the flaky comfort food with its own unique spin. Their signature biscuits are stacked high into sandwiches with names like the Squawking Goat, the Farmer, and the Five and Dime (a nod to a Jacksonville's 5 & Dime theatre company). You can also order platters of biscuits and gravy, waffles, and breakfast bowls fit for a champion. Other country favorites like collard greens, fried green tomatoes, and oatmeal finish off the menu. Quench your thirst on fresh-squeezed orange juice or freshly brewed coffee roasted in Jacksonville at Maple's own roasting facility. So, grab a seat, make a friend, and get a taste of Southern comfort food at this landmark restaurant founded right in the heart of Jacksonville that's quickly expanding its footprint throughout the country.

2004 San Marco Blvd.
(904) 398-1004
maplestreetbiscuits.com

GET TOGETHER
AT TOWN HALL

Fresh layered flavors, sustainable sourcing, and a decidedly West Coast aesthetic come together in this concept by two-time James Beard nominee Chef Tom Gray. Inspired by the desire to bring the community together over good food and drink, Town Hall is an intimate neighborhood destination situated in historic San Marco. Sourcing ingredients from local purveyors, each dish highlights the regional harvest in an elegant and sophisticated style complimented by fine wines from around the globe, local craft brews, and hand-mixed cocktails. Seared scallops, fresh Atlantic salmon, and duck breast are only a few of the favorites at Town Hall. Make sure to visit this local treasure, and savor each bite for yourself.

2012 San Marco Blvd.
(904) 398-0726
www.townhalljax.com

PUT A LITTLE SOUTH IN YOUR MOUTH
AT BEARDED PIG

Serving up succulent smoked meat along with homestyle fixins, Bearded Pig celebrates the timeless tradition of BBQ in a casual atmosphere complete with a festive beer garden. Bearded Pig makes good BBQ look easy when in reality it takes carefully researched technique, skill, and a whole lot of patience to master. Homestyle fixings may appear simple, but Southerners take their sides seriously, and competition is fierce. For these reasons, it's a major accomplishment to secure a coveted seat at the table of BBQ destinations in the South. Bearded Pig offers a modern yet casual vibe and is super family friendly. Kids will enjoy making their marks on the beer garden's chalk walls year-round, and water misters in the summer will keep them cool. Get your fill of pulled pork, smoked ribs, and jalapeno poppers, which join Southern favorites like Frito pie and pimento cheese on the menu.

1224 Kings Ave.
(904) 619-2247
thebeardedpigbbq.com

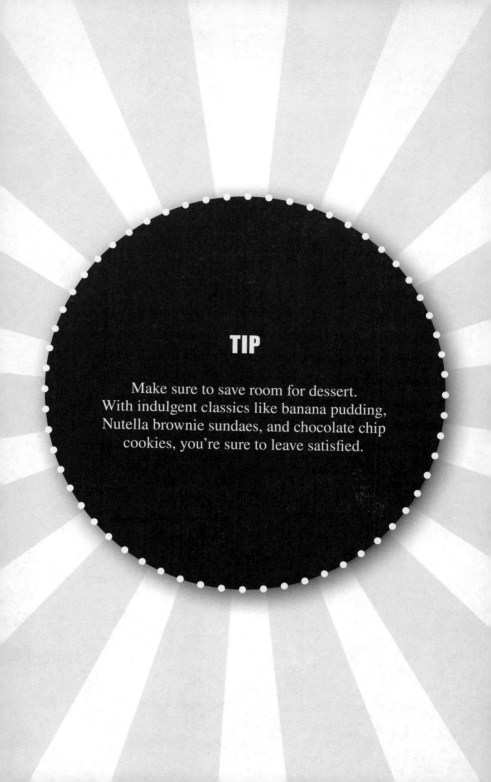

TIP

Make sure to save room for dessert.
With indulgent classics like banana pudding,
Nutella brownie sundaes, and chocolate chip
cookies, you're sure to leave satisfied.

MUSIC AND ENTERTAINMENT

CELEBRATE YOUR INDEPENDENCE
DURING 4TH OF JULY IN JAX BEACH

Jacksonville has its fair share of epic 4th of July celebrations, but none quite compare to the experience in Jacksonville Beach. It's nothing short of a spectacle as local revelers begin the festivities with an unofficial parade of beach cruisers decked out in red, white, and blue. Promptly at dark, fireworks explode from the Jacksonville Beach Fishing Pier in a kaleidoscope of colors and shapes. The fireworks rival any professional show and are always a marvel for young and old alike. It's a wonderfully unique celebration made special by the place it calls home, and it's simply not to be missed.

503 N. 1st St., Jacksonville Beach, FL 32250
www.jacksonvillebeach.org

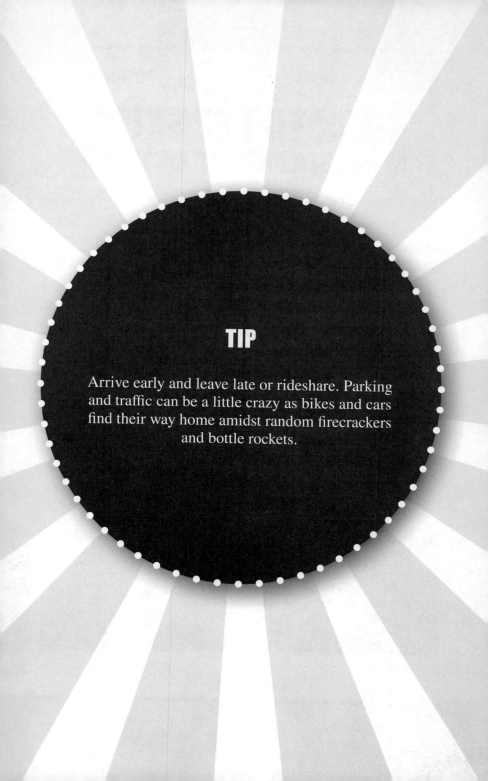

TIP

Arrive early and leave late or rideshare. Parking and traffic can be a little crazy as bikes and cars find their way home amidst random firecrackers and bottle rockets.

LOOK TO THE SKIES
AT THE SEA AND SKY AIR SHOW

Every other year, the sky above the Atlantic Ocean comes alive with a display of military precision and aeronautic ingenuity. Screaming across the sky at earth-rattling speeds, the Blue Angels and an all-star lineup of historic and modern aircraft make the Sea and Sky Air Show a free event that's fun for the whole family. Watch thrilling performances by both civilian and military flight teams, and experience live music, arts and crafts vendors, military vessels on an interactive display, plus a kids' play area. Bring your chairs, some shades, and a cool beverage to drink as you witness the skyline transformation during the Sea and Sky Air Show.

specialevents.coj.net/Special-Events/Sea-and-Sky-Airshow.aspx

TIP

Each year promises fun new surprises as the event's host rotates from Naval Air Station Jacksonville as "NAS Jacksonville Air Show" one year, to the City of Jacksonville's "Sea and Sky Air Show" at the beaches, creating more convenience for residents on opposing sides of the city and the delight of viewing the air show from the river or the sea.

ENJOY DINNER AND A SHOW
AT ALHAMBRA THEATRE AND DINING

As the longest-running dinner theatre in the nation, the Alhambra is a treasure to the Jacksonville community. Rescued from the brink of extinction in 2009, the Theatre has retained all of the iconic elements that make it unique while receiving some modern upgrades. The Alhambra is still well respected for quality performances provided in the 50-plus years it has been in operation. Boasting an impressive lineup of guest stars, the Alhambra has welcomed the likes of Morgan Fairchild, Barry Williams, and Betty Grable to its stage in addition to paving the way for countless burgeoning Broadway performers. The menu is unique to each show and prepared in the theatre's new kitchen, ensuring a quality fine-dining experience. The Alhambra has withstood the test of time and come out shining, so reserve a seat, enjoy your meal, and let the show begin!

12000 Beach Blvd.
(904) 641-1212
www.alhambrajax.com

DEMAND AN ENCORE
AT THE VETERANS MEMORIAL ARENA

Since its construction in 2003, the Veterans Memorial Arena has been "the" place to hook up with your closest 15,000 friends and give a cheer for your favorite artist or sports team. Home to the ECHL Icemen, NAL Jacksonville Sharks, and the ABA Jacksonville Giants, there is never a dull moment in this humidity-controlled colosseum. The acoustics have proven impressive as world-class legends such as Celine Dion, Elton John, and Cher have taken the stage to croon classic ballads and Top 40 hits. From Monster Jam to *Cirque du Soleil*, to Disney Princesses on Ice, the arena transforms from day to day into the fantasyland of our imaginations. It's hard not to smile, shout, cry, or laugh as you sing along with each artist during his or her riveting performance and—no doubt—cry out for an encore at the end.

300 A Philip Randolph Blvd.
(904) 630-3900
www.vystarveteransarena.com

CHILL OUT
AT THE JACKSONVILLE JAZZ FESTIVAL

For more than 40 years, Jacksonville has served as a mecca for jazz fans across the nation. What was begun in 1981 by Mayor Jake Godbold and Mike Tolbert as the Mayport and All That Jazz Festival has transformed into what we know today as the Jacksonville Jazz Festival. Each Memorial Day weekend, the musical sounds of jazz legends take over the urban core, cleverly nicknamed "Jazzville." As one of the largest free jazz festivals in the country, the Jacksonville Jazz Fest is a hub for art, culture, and those with a passion for jazz. With both free and VIP options, there is plenty to do throughout and around the festival, which has boasted headliners such as Miles Davis and Dizzy Gillespie and has helped to launch the careers of the likes of Harry Connick Jr. Join the Jacksonville Jazz Festival as one of the city's favorite traditions grows stronger—and louder—each year.

City of Jacksonville Events
(904) 255-5422
specialevents.coj.net

GET FOOTLOOSE
AT DANCIN' IN THE STREETS

As the main annual fundraiser for Beaches Town Center, the legendary Dancin' in the Streets festival has gained its own loyal following. For over 33 years, the community has come out *en masse* to celebrate the Town Center with shopping, imbibing, and (of course) dancing. A collective of artists from all over the city gathers to display and sell their handcrafted paintings, jewelry, pottery, blown glass, and more. As the region's favorite bands take the main stage, the sounds of upbeat tunes get people moving to the music with the lovely sweeping sands of the Atlantic Ocean in the background. It's a party passed on from generation to generation—and all for the continued improvement and beautification of this charming shopping center.

Beaches Town Center
200 1st St., Neptune Beach, FL 32266
(904) 241-1026
beachestowncenter.com/index.php

TAILGATE
BEFORE THE FLORIDA-GEORGIA GAME

Celebrate the famous Southern rivalry of the University of Florida and the University of Georgia at the world's largest cocktail party. Whether or not you're a football fan, you're sure to make some memories at this ultimate tailgate experience complete with barbecue, open bar, and sports memorabilia auction. Depending on your ticket, you can find tented seating areas, air-conditioned portable party hubs, and a myriad of food and beverage options. You'll discover old friends, make new ones, and enjoy the jesting (and roasting) born from generations of friendly rivalry while maybe rubbing shoulders with a celebrity or two. Don your blue and orange or red and black and embrace the Florida- Georgia takeover that swamps Jacksonville every year. It's a party you won't soon forget.

Tailgater's Parking: First and Ten Lot
1906 E. Beaver St.
(800) 685-7618
www.gtepresents.com

LISTEN UP
AT THE BLUE JAY LISTENING ROOM

If anyone understands the power of music to move and heal the human soul, it's Cara Burky, the creator of Blue Jay Listening Room. It was her dream to establish an intimate space for songwriters and musicians to come and share what's sacred. Blue Jay is a space to be mindful and to hear the tales behind the songs, learn where the soulful lyrics had their origins, and be inspired to write your own songs as well. Instead of a venue where musicians are trying to play over the noise of the crowd in a packed bar or club, Blue Jay provides a comfortable oasis that is conducive to listening. At Blue Jay, you'll find a community of like-minded music lovers prepared to give their complete attention to the impassioned artists appearing under the spotlight. Arrive early, order a glass of wine or craft beer, and settle in for a listen as you enjoy a night at the Blue Jay Listening Room.

2457 3rd St. South, Jacksonville Beach, FL 32250
(904) 318-3020
www.bluejayjax.com

TIP

Blue Jay provides business cards for listeners who may need to Uber home. Just put the card in your dashboard, and you don't have to worry about being towed.

LAUGH OUT LOUD
AT THE FLORIDA THEATRE

Since its grand opening in 1927, the Florida Theatre has been an icon in the Jacksonville community—a welcome palace of escape. Designed to be the largest theatre of its kind in Florida, in its heyday the Theatre welcomed guests daily, and couples could enjoy a date and childcare for around $1.50 a night. The Theatre also boasted a rooftop garden where couples could enjoy a night of dancing and live music after the programmed entertainment. Today, you'll be hard-pressed to find a venue in Jax with such robust acoustics or the pedigree of performers who have led the way, including Elvis himself. Today, more than 200 performances grace the stage annually, including comedy, ballet, opera, children's shows, and community programs. Lovingly preserved through time, the Florida Theatre looks much the same as it did upon its opening nearly a century ago. The "Palace of Dreams" will overwhelm you with its stately presence and warm embrace, and the entertainment is sure to provide you a welcome escape from the realities of your daily grind.

128 E. Forsyth St., Suite 300
(904) 355-5661
floridatheatre.com

START THANKSGIVING
AT PETE'S BAR

In an ever-changing world, it's nice to know that some things really do stay the same. Such is the case with Pete's Bar in Neptune Beach. This late-night watering hole is still home to 25¢ pool tables, $1 foosball games, and affordable drinks. It's the kind of place that invites you to come as you are and unwind with old friends as only a neighborhood bar can do. In its 80-plus years in existence, Pete's has given the community its share of fun—but none greater than the tradition of gathering at the bar on Thanksgiving morning. For decades, crowds have gathered together while donning their most colorful Thanksgiving attire to share a toast and revelry with friends, family, and beloved neighbors. Visitors come from near and far to join in the tradition, some quenching their thirst after a turkey trot and some killing time while their feast is in the oven. It's a fun way to kick off the holiday season and an experience everyone should have at least once.

117 1st St., Neptune Beach, FL 32266
(904) 249-9158
petesbarjax.com

TIP
Don't forget to stop at an ATM. Pete's bar is cash only.

JAM ON
AT PORCHFEST

Each November, Jacksonville's historic Springfield neighborhood echoes with the sounds of live music during Porchfest. Crowds gather to enjoy some of the region's most talented musicians as they perform from the porches of charming bungalows and stately Victorians in this neighborhood just north of downtown Jacksonville. Streets are closed for this free family- and pet-friendly block party event that celebrates the revival of the once-distressed neighborhood that is now returning to its former glory. Food trucks line the streets offering refreshments to the gathered music fans while vendors showcase their artisan crafts for purchase. It's a colorful bazaar set in the heart of one of Jacksonville's oldest neighborhoods, and sponsorships from the event go to benefit future arts programming in Springfield. Bring a blanket and chairs; camp out next to your favorite porch; and embrace the sights, sounds, and soul of one of Jacksonville's most-beloved neighborhoods when you attend Porchfest.

204 W. 3rd St.
(904) 353-7727
www.jacksonvilleporchfest.org

WATCH A SILVER SCREEN CLASSIC
AT SAN MARCO THEATRE

Designed by the well-known architect who also crafted the Florida Theatre, San Marco Theatre is another rare jewel that has survived the test of time. Constructed in 1938 by Roy Benjamin, San Marco Theatre shines with an Art Deco motif. Situated in the heart of San Marco's shopping district, it's surrounded by boutiques and restaurants, making it the perfect date night out. Visitors will find a mixture of current blockbusters and silver screen classics on the marquee, keeping movie lovers guessing about what will be playing next. Leveling up from the classic movie concession fare, San Marco Theatre offers more robust menu items such as freshly made pizza, sandwiches, and a fine selection of beer and wine. It's an iconic piece of Jacksonville's history and a perfect place to enjoy an experience you'll only find here on the First Coast.

1996 San Marco Blvd.
Movie Line (904) 396-4845
Business Office (904) 396-5130
www.sanmarcotheatre.com

LISTEN TO BLUES ON THE BEACH
AT SPRINGING THE BLUES

Every spring since 1990, the blues change the tempo in the heart of Jacksonville Beach. Springing the Blues is a tradition that kicks off the warm-weather season and welcomes young and old to don their sunglasses and tap their toes to the rhythm offered up by world-class blues musicians. As a free outdoor event, Springing the Blues is the perfect place to meet up with your friends and enjoy a day jamming out to music by your favorite artists. For additional entertainment, there are food trucks, shopping, and a kids' area, plus the Atlantic Ocean beckons merely steps away from the main stage. Enjoy three days of blues, beach, and the best of Florida weather at Springing the Blues.

1st St. North, Jacksonville Beach, FL 32250
(904) 270-9301
www.springingtheblues.com

TIP
If you're a general admission attendee, don't forget to bring some folding chairs or a blanket to relax on.

SCREEN AN INDIE
AT SUN-RAY CINEMA

If you're looking for a historic theatre with hip ambiance and a penchant for screening indie films, you'll find just that at Sun-Ray Cinema. Housed in a 1920s structure that was originally built to show the first "talking pictures" of its time, today, this dual-screen cinema has taken on a life of its own in the artsy Five Points Riverside neighborhood it calls home. In addition to reopening the cinema as "Sun-Ray Cinema" a decade ago, the owners recently added a pizza joint lovingly called the Pizza Cave!, serving up pies and good times. Did I mention the entire interior is designed as a facsimile of a Florida cavern? Back in the cinema, you can order pizza, popcorn, wine, beer, and other favorite movie snacks and have them delivered right to your seat as you take in the latest offbeat flick or mainstream blockbuster.

1028 Park St.
(904) 359-0049
www.sunraycinema.com

VOLUNTEER
AT THEATRE JACKSONVILLE

Since its inception in 1919, Theatre Jacksonville has served as a community resource for culture and entertainment. With continuously running seasons for 100 years and counting, this volunteer-based center for theatre arts has stood the test of time and is widely recognized as one of the oldest continuously running community theatres in the nation. Theatre Jacksonville sits in the middle of historic San Marco and welcomes young and old to be transported through the art of storytelling. With programs for adults and students alike, the theatre is invested in enriching the lives of its community. In fact, since 1972 the theatre has been named Jacksonville's official theatre. As a community nonprofit, Theatre Jacksonville's support staff is made up of just that: members of its community. While seeing a show is certainly considered a "must do," I also recommend volunteering. There are a host of roles to play as a volunteer, including usher, set builder, set painter, lighting technician, and more. Support a Jacksonville institution by being a part of Theatre Jacksonville.

2032 San Marco Blvd.
(904) 396-4425
www.theatrejax.com

TRAVERSE THE GLOBE
AT THE WORLD OF
NATIONS CELEBRATION

There's no quicker way to traverse cultures across this lonely planet than by visiting the annual World of Nations festival here in the Bold New City of the South. A celebration of diversity across cultures, the World of Nations festival was established in 1993 as an opportunity to showcase the variety of diverse international communities that comprise the region. Countries historically represented at the festival range from Cambodia to Ethiopia and the Philippines. Experience food from around the globe, live music presentations, and displays of cultures both familiar and foreign, plus an interactive play area just for kids. Taste new food, shop for handmade artisan crafts, and don your native folk attire for this weekend that recognizes our origins and how that makes us unique.

904-255-8008
specialevents.coj.net

WATCH THE SHOWDOWN UNFOLD
AT FISH TO FORK

Seafood lovers searching for a true "dock to dish" culinary experience need to look no further than Omni Amelia Island Resort's annual Fish to Fork Weekend. This three-day extravaganza gathers award-winning chefs from near and far to compete in a Food Network-style battle of the knives as chefs catch and cook their harvest from the sea. The weekend culminates at the Saturday night Main Event, where each chef prepares a unique dish complete with a signature cocktail while the attendees vote for their favorite preparation. During the voting process, the talent divides into teams to face off in a group challenge featuring a secret ingredient. It's a lively gathering under the shade of the resort's stately live oaks featuring a generous buffet, open bar, live music, and plenty of food-loving company. Come hungry—you will certainly leave full!

39 Beach Lagoon Rd., Fernandina Beach, FL 32034
(904) 261-6161
www.omnihotels.com/hotels/amelia-island-plantation

BECOME A SANDCASTLE ARTISAN
AT OPENING OF THE BEACHES

Stormtroopers, Vikings, flamingos, and ballerinas, oh my! For almost a century, the beaches have celebrated their official welcome to warm weather with an eclectic parade of characters from around the community. Candy and beads are thrown to outstretched eager young hands as performers in handmade floats roll by to the sounds of bandstand favorites and modern-day hits. It's an animated display of diverse community voices coming together to celebrate what makes the beaches stand out. Headlining the event are live music performances at the Beaches Pavilion and the much-anticipated sandcastle-making competition. Teams show off their sand-wielding skills as they let their imaginations fly with a little bit of sand, water, and determination. It's a tradition that's been passed down from generation to generation as the beaches have grown from small humble neighborhoods to a thriving community and travel destination. And it's an event the public is warmly invited to be a part of.

Downtown Jacksonville Beach
(904) 247-6100
www.jacksonvillebeach.org

GO BEHIND THE SCENES
AT SALLY DARK RIDES

Perhaps one of the best kept secrets in Jacksonville, Sally Dark Rides has been creating turnkey dark rides and animatronics right here on the First Coast for more than 30 years. These rides go on to be memorable experiences and traditions for families around the globe at theme parks and museums. On a dark ride, visitors take amusement park funhouse-style rides through animated scenes from their favorite movies and books to get up-close experiences with iconic characters. On behind-the-scenes tours, you'll see the technology behind the robots and the skill it takes to craft the realistic-looking bodies those robots inhabit. Sally Dark Rides is indeed a gem on the First Coast and an attraction everyone should plan to experience.

745 W. Forsyth St.
(904) 355-7100
www.sallydarkrides.com

TIP

Although tours are free, reservations are required with a minimum age for guests of seven years old due to thematic elements.

SPORTS AND RECREATION

MAKE A SPLASH
AT ADVENTURE LANDING

With over five million visitors since its inception in 1995, Adventure Landing knows a thing or two about the serious business of having fun. Now with family entertainment centers spread throughout the states, Adventure Landing is proud to boast Jacksonville Beach as its flagship location. An arcade, go-karts, and laser tag provide ample entertainment for the whole family year-round. However, in the summer, Adventure Landing's largest attraction, Shipwreck Island Water Park, invites revelers to cool off and make a splash. Shipwreck Island is home to four extreme slides, a lazy river, and a 500,000-gallon wave pool. Beachgoers have only a short distance to go to reach Shipwreck Island's thrilling attractions, with the added bonus of not having to shake the sand out of your towels. When your water adventure comes to an end, refuel at one of the snack bars, and finish your day with a game of miniature golf. With so many choices, you can be sure that whichever amusement you choose, you'll leave with enough treasured memories to last a lifetime.

1944 Beach Blvd., Jacksonville Beach, FL 32250
(904) 246-4386
jacksonville-beach.adventurelanding.com

THRILL TO AN AIRBOAT ADVENTURE
WITH SEA SERPENT TOURS

The airboat was invented in 1905 by none other than Alexander Graham Bell, the same famous inventor credited with the telephone. Air-boating has a long tradition in the low country and swamplands of the South. Skimming along the shallow surface of the water, an airboat ride is an ideal way to get up close to nature. Sea Serpent Tours take passengers on a guided treasure hunt through passages of time and water on their state-of-the-art custom airboats. As you troll through the murky waters of the St. Johns River's tributary creeks, you'll enjoy a personal narration of the region's rich nautical history, including the story of a greedy pirate who ultimately met his demise near the Jacksonville shoreline. It's an interactive adventure with plenty of photo ops and a mix of backwoods cruising and high-speed action. Witness gators, turtles, wild boar, and waterfowl in their natural habitat, all from the safety of the mighty *Sea Dragon* or *Sea Serpent* airboats.

6550 SR 13 N., St Augustine, FL 32092
(904) 495-4200
www.seaserpenttours.com

FIND RENEWAL IN NATURE
AT JACKSONVILLE
ARBORETUM & GARDENS

What was once a strip mine for minerals used to create titanium is now a 120-acre woodland that serves as a center for natural renewal. As the land heals itself, so it does with the human soul. Jacksonville Arboretum & Gardens is a space to observe and study the natural plant life native to our region. Choose from seven different trails to explore, and lose yourself in the wonder of nature. In your wanderings, be introduced to over 100 labeled native plants like stevia, aloe, avocado, prickly pear, and ragweed. At the center of it all, you'll encounter a large two-acre lake ideal for reflecting, photography, and the observation of wildlife. There's no excuse needed to get in touch with nature, but the Arboretum provides plenty of encouragement as it hosts several events each year, including butterfly releases, open-air painting festivities, and food- and beverage-inspired gatherings.

1445 Millcoe Rd.
(904) 318-4342
www.jacksonvillearboretum.org

TIP

The Jacksonville Arboretum is open seven days a week and is pet- and child-friendly. Although there is no fee required to enter, a donation of $3 per guest is suggested.

BIKE
THE BALDWIN RAIL TRAIL

Formerly an abandoned CSX railroad corridor, the Baldwin Rail Trail joins the federal initiative to convert abandoned railways into linear park systems. As one of the oldest Florida trails initiated in the Rails to Trails program, the Baldwin Rail Trail offers nearly 14 miles of paved road dedicated for use by cyclists, walkers, and inline skaters. In addition to the paved path, a parallel unpaved trail is available for equestrian use. The Baldwin Rail Trail runs through the heart of Camp Milton Historic Preserve, a former Civil War encampment, plus there are several additional trailheads located just off the asphalt path for day hiking and horseback riding. The trail enjoys a canopy of shade for much of the almost 15 miles and is a great location for spotting Florida wildlife.

850 Center St. N., Baldwin, FL 32234
(904) 630-2489
www.coj.net

TIP
Restrooms and water stops are available along the path, as are benches for resting.

PLAY LIKE A CHAMPION
AT THE PLAYERS STADIUM COURSE

World renowned as the home of THE PLAYERS Championship, TPC Sawgrass is where champions go to win. Where better place to rise to the challenge than on THE PLAYERS own home turf, the Stadium Course. As one of two courses at TPC Sawgrass, the Stadium Course is the first of its kind. Designed with the fans in mind, the green rises and falls around each hole to accommodate the masses that flock to see THE PLAYERS each year. Consistently ranked one of the top courses to play in the states, the Stadium's well-known turf attracts golfers from near and far. Accept the challenge of the iconic 17th hole, the Island Green, as you try to hit one of the most difficult par 3s in the game. It's a championship-caliber golf course open to all players, so be sure to add it to your bucket list while here on the First Coast.

110 Championship Way, Ponte Vedra Beach, FL 32082
(904) 273-3235
tpc.com/sawgrass/the-players-stadium-course

HUNT FOR SHARKS' TEETH
AT GUANA RESERVE'S MIDDLE BEACH

From white sands to pink coquina, the beaches in North Florida are as diverse as they are rich in beauty. Each shoreline has its charms, but if you are looking for a slower pace where the foot traffic is minimal, head to the private sands of Guana Reserve's Middle Beach. A short trip down the boardwalk leads you over and down the massive sweeping dunes of the reserve. In fact, the dune system is as large as the ones for which the West Coast is famous. Because of its unique topography and low traffic, Middle Beach provides a stunning landscape for wildlife to call home. Naturally, photographers flock to the area to capture the elegant beauty of the beach and dunes, and families spend memorable quality time together in one of the region's most treasured natural sanctuaries. If you happen to be on the lookout for sharks' teeth or unique shells, bring a bucket for collecting as Middle Beach is also a treasure hunter's dream.

1641-1799 A1A Scenic and Historic Coastal Byway
Ponte Vedra Beach, FL 32082
(904) 823-4500, gtmnerr.org

TIP
Remember to bring cash; parking is $3.

GO CAMPING
AT KATHRYN ABBEY HANNA PARK

With 1 1/2 miles of sandy beaches, 20 miles of hiking and biking trails, and a 60-acre lake for kayaking or fishing, Hanna Park has more than enough attractions to draw outdoor enthusiasts. Tucked away within her borders is the beach's best surfing spot, the Poles, along with an interactive playground for kids to explore. Offering 300 wooded campsites including tent sites, RV parking, and rustic cabins, the park invites visitors to stay awhile and immerse themselves in nature. Even furry friends are welcome in Hanna Park, giving you all the more reason to spend some time in this well-preserved, mature, coastal hammock.

500 Wonderwood Dr., Atlantic Beach, FL 32233
(904) 249-4700
hannapark@coj.net

TIP
Parking in Hanna Park is $5 per carload.

DRIVE ON THE BEACH
AT HUGUENOT MEMORIAL PARK

Named after the brave explorers who fled France for the New World with hopes of religious freedom, Huguenot Park today serves as a refuge for seabirds and endangered marine animals. Surrounded by three bodies of water, Huguenot is one of the few on the First Coast to which you can drive and park your car. With views of the St. Johns River, the Atlantic Ocean, and Fort George Inlet, there is plenty of natural beauty to feast your eyes on. Visitors enjoy waterfront campsites, playgrounds, and trails for walking and riding bikes. Go birding, surf the waves, or enjoy fishing along the shores for hours of leisurely fun. It's a great place to unwind, celebrate, and spend the day relaxing on the beach. Arrive early on holidays like Memorial Day and the 4th of July; it gets packed!

10980 Heckscher Dr.
(904) 255-4255
www.coj.net

TIP

Rookies beware: cars are swallowed by the tide every day. Keep your eyes on the tide; it rises fast.

GET HORSEY
AT THE JACKSONVILLE EQUESTRIAN CENTER

In case you mistook Kentucky as the only state known for its horses, think again. Florida is home to many fine equestrians. In fact, the Sunshine State is well known as home base for competitors who spend their winters in the South to continue training. As such, the Jacksonville Equestrian Center has been a welcome addition to the city. This $30 million facility plays host to equestrian events such as USDF Regional Qualifying and Region 3 Dressage Finals as well as a diverse range of community events. Come and watch these fine athletes show off their skills in one of several arenas that include indoor, outdoor, turf, and jumping rings. If you plan on staying a while and camping during a competition, you'll also be pleased to explore the miles of hiking and biking trails located around the facility.

13611 Normandy Blvd.
(904) 255-4254
www.jaxequestriancenter.com

BEAT FEET
AT THE GATE RIVER RUN

With more than 20,000 participants, the Gate River Run is the nation's largest 15K race. Operating for over four decades, the River Run spans multiple bridges over the St. Johns River and is the official USA 15K Championship. It's a festive affair with a multiday expo and plenty of family-friendly events. If you aren't into long-distance running, try the 5K, or cheer on the kids for the Junior Run or Diaper Dash! Live bands are situated along the route to keep the momentum going strong, and the energy of the crowd propels each participant forward. As you complete your run, join the celebration with over 120 kegs of beer provided for the crowd, in addition to healthy fare provided by Publix. With more prize money handed out than for any other 15K race, there are plenty of reasons to join the run.

E. Duval St.

gateriverrun15k.com

TIP
In addition, each participant receives a T-shirt while finishers receive commemorative medals.

EXPLORE
SKELETON BEACH

Mother Nature certainly has an imagination, and Skeleton Beach is living proof. Load your car for the short journey from Mayport to Heckscher Drive on the St. Johns River Ferry, and enjoy a scenic drive from there through the Ft. George and Talbot Island Forests to Big Talbot Island. Park and hike an easy trail to Skeleton Beach. Unlike any other beach in North Florida, years of erosion have collapsed part of the forest of giant oaks. They find their final resting place now on the white sands of Big Talbot Island overlooking Nassau Sound. This remote landscape will captivate you with its other-worldly silhouettes. Children of all ages can't help but turn the salt-preserved limbs into giant jungle gyms, and photographers of all genres flock to the beach in attempts to capture its wonder. Make sure to pack a picnic and embrace the solitude and majesty of this iconic destination.

Big Talbot Island State Park
12157 Heckscher Dr.
www.coj.net/departments/parks-and-recreation/recreation-and-community-programming/parks/big-talbot-island-state-park

TIP
Remember to bring cash to pay for parking.

SUPPORT DU-U-U-UVAL
AT A JACKSONVILLE JAGUARS GAME

More than a quarter of a century after the Jacksonville Jaguars became an NFL team, the Bold City keeps on roaring its support. Jax's home team has had a wild ride and continues to surprise, defy, and rise above the odds, thanks in large part to the support of its fans in the community. With a presence on both sides of the pond, the Jags also play in London every year. For better or for worse, fans on the First Coast fill up the stands to root for their home team and enjoy one of the most festive game-day experiences in the league. The stadium even has two pools and cabana seating to keep fans cool on the hottest of game days. Access to a Jags game also gives you free admission to a giant fan party above the north end zone. It's here you'll find DJs, unique concessions, and signature cocktails that will ensure that, win or lose, you have the time of your life.

1 TIAA Bank Field Dr.
Ticket office: (904) 633-2000
www.jaguars.com

FINISH
THE DONNA

After being diagnosed with breast cancer for the second time, award-winning news anchor Donna Deegan founded the Donna Foundation to bring aid to families struggling with the challenges of breast cancer, as well as contributing to research focused on eradicating the disease. Recognized by CNN as one of the top marathons "Worth the Trip," 26.2 with Donna was founded in 2008 and has been named the National Marathon to Finish Breast Cancer. Runners decked out in various shades of pink wind their way through some of Northeast Florida's most beautiful coastline. Ranked one of the fastest marathons in Florida, the Donna has earned the status of Boston Marathon Qualifier and is an achievement worth vying for. With an average temperature of 55 degrees, February is the perfect time of year to don your pink and run for a cause.

The DONNA Foundation
11762 Marco Beach Dr., Suite 6
(904) 355-PINK (7465)
breastcancermarathon.com

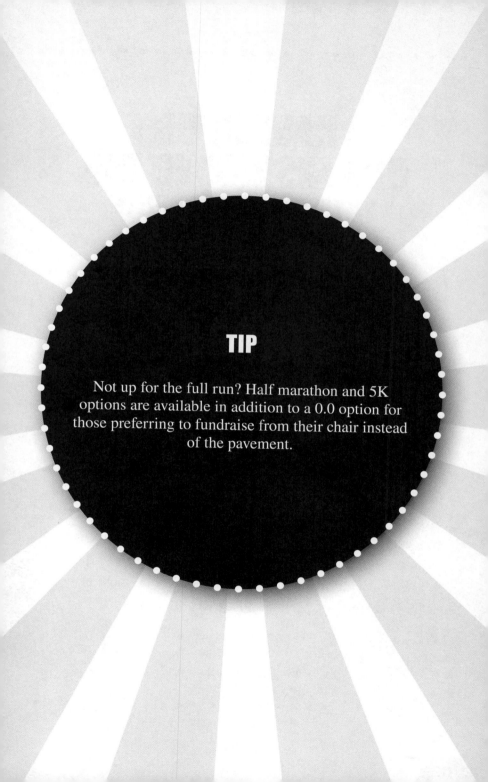

TIP

Not up for the full run? Half marathon and 5K options are available in addition to a 0.0 option for those preferring to fundraise from their chair instead of the pavement.

HAVE GOOD OLD-FASHIONED FUN
WITH THE JACKSONVILLE JUMBO SHRIMP

Looking for affordable fun for the whole family on a Friday night? For as little as $5 a ticket, the Jacksonville Jumbo Shrimp are the answer. Jacksonville's AA minor league team carries on the timeless tradition of America's favorite pastime as fans gather every April through August for good old-fashioned fun. There isn't a bad seat anywhere among the 11,000 situated in the 121 Financial Ballpark. Enjoy high-visibility sightlines and HD viewing screens for wherever you decide to roam during the game-day experience. In fact, all tickets can access the air-conditioned Wheelhouse Lounge and a variety of local-inspired fare. Featuring three Sky Decks, Budweiser Tiki Terrace and Wolfson Children's Hospital Kids Zone, there is plenty to keep you entertained during all nine innings. Just be sure to stick around after the game: you won't want to miss the fireworks following each Friday home game in addition to more elaborate displays celebrating Memorial Day and 4th of July.

301 A Philip Randolph Blvd.
(904) 358-2846
www.milb.com/jacksonville

CATCH THE BIG ONE
OFF JACKSONVILLE
BEACH FISHING PIER

Hurricanes have had their heyday with Jacksonville's fishing piers, including the most recent installment in North Jacksonville Beach. In 2016, Hurricane Matthew took off half of the 1,300-foot fishing pier, leaving it around a quarter mile long and still operational before reconstruction began in 2019. For only $3 a day, fishermen can nab a spot on the rail and relax in the sunshine while baiting their hooks for the Atlantic's harvest. Well-known catches include redfish, tarpon, black drum, and sheepshead, but it's not uncommon to also catch a ray or shark. Beachgoers not interested in fishing can also enjoy a walk over the water, with a bird's-eye perspective for people watching at just $1 per person. Afterward, take a stroll on the boardwalk, pop into a cantina for chips and salsa, or head to the Seawalk Pavilion on a festival day for live music.

503 N. 1st St., Jacksonville Beach, FL 32250
(904) 241-1515
www.jacksonvillebeach.org

ATTEND
THE PLAYERS CHAMPIONSHIP

Every year, thousands of spectators gather in Ponte Vedra Beach to witness one of golf's most prestigious tournaments, THE PLAYERS Championship. With the largest prize of any golf tournament, THE PLAYERS draws upon the sport's top athletes to vie for the $15 million purse. THE PLAYERS Stadium Course was designed with not only the golfers but the fans in mind. Theatre-style slopes surround the course, giving fans unobstructed sightlines of their favorite players. And you don't have to be a hard-core golf fanatic to have a good time—THE PLAYERS is a stylish and interactive affair for golf fans with plenty to engage and inspire attendees of every age and interest. Rock the latest spring fashions, make new friends, and catch up with old ones as you dine on food from some of Jacksonville's best culinary destinations. Don't forget to take your turn at the 17th Hole Challenge experience, a replica of the world-famous Island Green 17th hole, to see how you stack up against the champs,and then swing by (pun intended!) the massive PGA TOUR Fan Shop to purchase some exclusive merch.

TPC
110 TPC Blvd., Ponte Vedra Beach, FL 32082
(833) 888-6227
www.tpc.com

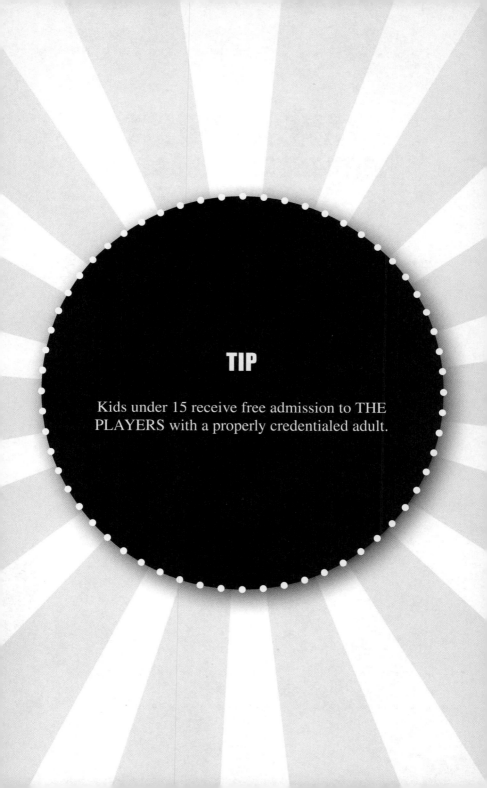

TIP

Kids under 15 receive free admission to THE PLAYERS with a properly credentialed adult.

TAKE A CRUISE
WITH THE ST. JOHNS RIVER
TAXI AND TOURS

For a unique view of Jacksonville's skyline, head to the water. With transport to and from destinations and hotels along the St. Johns River as well as private charters, the River Taxi has become the quintessential way to experience the River City's famous waterway. Feel free to BYOB for the sunset tour that includes live music and sweeping views of the city at dusk, or enjoy a narrated tour of Jacksonville's history and best-kept secrets. See if you can pick out some of the city's famous landmarks such as the Friendship Fountain, the Museum of Science and History, or TIAA Bank Field (home of the Jaguars) as you enjoy your cruise down the river. Attending an event downtown? The River Taxi is a great way to arrive at your destination along the water's edge while avoiding the stress of traffic.

1015 Museum Cir.
(904) 860-8294
www.jaxrivertaxi.com

HAVE A SPA DAY
AT THE RITZ-CARLTON

Treat yourself to some serious therapy at one of the finest day spas in North Florida. The Spa at The Ritz-Carlton, Amelia Island, offers luxury facilities and wellness amenities designed to put you at ease and bring balance in an increasingly stressful world. With access to both the fitness center and private spa pool deck, you don't have to stay overnight to enjoy all the resort has to offer. Come for a single treatment or for a complete day of relaxation, and experience the excellence in service that is distinctly Ritz-Carlton. Signature services include a variety of techniques and therapeutic modalities that ensure that each unique service not only spirits you away to a more relaxed mindset but also connects you to the elegant elements around you in this coastal retreat. Whether your personal treatment involves the Heaven in a Hammock massage, Honey Butter wrap, or Enzyme Renewal facial, you'll surely leave refreshed and recharged.

4750 Amelia Island Parkway, Amelia Island, FL 32034
(904) 277-1100
www.ritzcarlton.com/en/hotels/florida/amelia-island/spa

STAND-UP PADDLEBOARD
AT JAX SURF AND PADDLE

Jacksonville is referred to as the First Coast due to its situation at the top of Florida's eastern coastline along the Atlantic Ocean. In addition to shoreline, we also boast miles of Intracoastal Waterway, marshland, and the St. Johns River. Blessed with nearly year-round temperate conditions, there couldn't be a better excuse to get on the water. The beaches are teeming with opportunities to do just that, and Jax Surf and Paddle are the go-to experts who can help you find your sea legs. Whether you're just learning or more experienced, you'll find everything you need to get you on your way at Jax Surf and Paddle in Neptune Beach. Enjoy a guided stand-up paddleboard eco-tour through the Intracoastal Waterway, take private surfing lessons, sign up for a fitness class, or rent the equipment you need to shred the waves. The ocean's waiting; get out there.

241 Atlantic Blvd. #102, Neptune Beach, FL 32266
(904) 372-9083
jacksonvillesurfandpaddle.com

Photo courtesy of Ryan Ketterman

CULTURE AND HISTORY

WALK THROUGH HISTORY
AT THE BEACHES MUSEUM

Jacksonville's beaches attract thousands of visitors every year, and it's easy to see why. As you make the journey over the intracoastal bridges to the island that the beach communities call home, you almost immediately feel at ease. The laid-back sense of island time gives folks plenty of reason to find a beach home of their own and settle down in one of the casual villages along North Florida's coastline. The Beaches Museum tells the story of these communities' first pioneers. In the main building, you can explore permanent and traveling exhibits that tell the tale of how the original settlers made a life here. Explore the archives, and read historical accounts of hope in the midst of natural disasters and the stories of how the beaches persevered through the Civil Rights movements, the Industrial Revolution, and two World Wars. The museum becomes even more interactive as you stroll through History Park, where you'll find historical buildings dating back to the late 1800s as well as a train engine from 1911. A visit to the Beaches Museum is an eye-opening experience and one that celebrates what makes Jacksonville's beaches so unique.

381 Beach Blvd., Jacksonville Beach, FL 32250
(904) 241-5657
www.beachesmuseum.org

TIP

Admission to the Beaches Museum
is free for all ages.

ORDER TAPAS ON THE ROOFTOP
AT THE CASA MARINA HOTEL

A classic never goes out of style, and so it is with the Casa Marina Hotel. A Jacksonville Beach icon, the Casa Marina opened in 1925 when the glamour of the beaches was at its height. This Spanish-style structure paints a unique silhouette and is just steps away from the Jacksonville Beach Fishing Pier. Stay for a night in one of the individually decorated rooms, or just stop by for a cocktail and tapas in the Penthouse Rooftop Bar. From the rooftop, enjoy panoramic views of the pier and the wide expanse of shoreline. The Casa Marina hosts its fair share of events, and an evening in the courtyard dancing under the stars is not to be missed. It's a legendary destination and one the beaches' residents are proud to preserve for generations to come.

691 N. 1st St., Jacksonville Beach, FL 32250
(904) 270-0025
casamarinahotel.com

ADMIRE THE LUXURY
AT *CONCOURS D'ELEGANCE*

Every spring, The Ritz-Carlton, Amelia Island, hosts the *Concours d'Elegance*, a luxury car show known for its sophistication and significant charitable donations since its inception in 1996. The *Concours d'Elegance* is a multiday event with a variety of interactive experiences from fashion shows and winemakers' dinners to auctions, book signings, and the competition itself. The event culminates with recognition and awards for Best in Show, Best in Class, and Corporate Awards. Each year, the *Concours* also honors an outstanding person in the automotive industry, showcasing him or her on the event's marque. Elegant models dress up in period ensembles to match the era of the vehicles on display, and celebrity sightings are common. One of the most luxurious automotive events in the industry, it's a feast for the eyes, and it happens annually right here on the First Coast.

750 Amelia Island Pkwy., Amelia Island, FL 32034
(904) 636-0027
www.ameliaconcours.org

ATTEND A NIGHT FEEDING
AT CATTY SHACK RANCH

Open to the public since 2004, Catty Shack Ranch was established as a rescue, rehabilitation, and forever home for endangered big cats. A volunteer-driven, nonprofit charity, part of Catty Shack's mission is to educate the public about the plight of these big cats in the wild and in captivity. A visit to Catty Shack includes a tour throughout the facility and an introduction to the history and purpose behind the rescue. Visit the residents, and meander through the grounds as you get to know the lions, tigers, panthers, foxes, and coatimundis. As a top-rated attraction in Jacksonville, these animals are beloved by all, and Catty Shack encourages all the photos you like.

1860 Starratt Rd.
(904) 757-3603
cattyshack.org

TIP

Be sure to experience the highly rated night feedings, where you'll witness these nocturnal animals really come alive as they are fed around 600 pounds of meat for dinner.

CATCH AN OPEN HOUSE
AT CoRK ART DISTRICT

Perhaps one of Jacksonville's best-kept secrets is that it is a thriving hub for the arts. With an annual art festival and not one but two art districts, the art culture in Jax is best described as diverse, innovative, and fresh. One such district is located on the corner of Rosselle and King Streets—hence the name CoRK. Here in this pioneering enclave, artists have created spaces that they consider their second homes. At CoRK, craftspeople work in diverse mediums to create and market their art. From photography to sculpting and watercolors to charcoal, you'll find a new medium around every corner and meet the artists behind each masterpiece when you attend one of their events.

2689 Rosselle St.
corkartsdistrict.com

TIP
CoRK is not generally open to the public, so keep an eye out for their events for a chance to get a peek inside the process.

TAKE A HIKE
AT FORT CAROLINE
NATIONAL MEMORIAL

The Timucuan Ecological Historical Preserve is an outdoor wonderland in Jacksonville consisting of 46,000 acres of marshland, coastal hammock, forest, and shoreline. The range is large, but you'll find the visitor center for the preserve located at Fort Caroline. Traverse the timeline of history as you learn about the importance of the wetlands to North Florida's inhabitants over the last several centuries as well as glean important facts about the rise and fall of Fort Caroline and the brave settlers who were destined for a tragic demise. A visit is not complete without a stop at the Ribault Monument, where you'll take in an epic view of the St. Johns River from St. Johns Bluff. Bring the whole family, hike the trails, and visit the replica of Fort Caroline for a glimpse into what life was like in the 1500s.

12713 Fort Caroline Rd.
(904) 641-7155
www.nps.gov

DO YOUR RESEARCH
AT THE JACKSONVILLE
LIBRARY MAIN BRANCH

Since its inception in 1878, the Jacksonville Library's Main Branch has called no fewer than five locations its home. One building even met its demise in the famous Great Fire of 1901 that reduced much of the Bold City to ash. The Carnegie Library was rebuilt afterward, funded with $50,000 from Andrew Carnegie himself. Times, trends, and interests changed over the generations, but the city's commitment to the library only grew. Today, the Main Branch is situated on Laura St. downtown, steps away from the Museum of Modern Art and Jacksonville's Hemming Plaza. It's a stately building that serves as the main centerpiece for the Jacksonville library system. There is ample space for events, enrichments, and hundreds of computers for public access. The stone structure houses four floors of books, and a serene outdoor courtyard has a fountain for strolling or quiet reading.

303 Laura St. N.
(904) 255-2665
www.jaxpubliclibrary.org

TIP
Don't miss the children's section full of dynamic titles that will enrich young readers' minds.

CROSS THE RIVER
ON THE ST. JOHNS RIVER FERRY

Connecting Mayport Village and Fort George Island, the St. Johns River Ferry transports automobiles, pedestrians, and cyclists on a short and pleasant cruise across the St. Johns River. Leaving on the half hour, the ferry is a local favorite among day trippers and families, shortening the trip from the beaches to Huguenot Park, the Talbot Islands, and Amelia Island. There's something about the nautical tradition of passing over water that brings an immediate sense of getting away, and the short ride is a simple way to let your worries fade into the background. Kids are eager to experience the brief transition from shore to shore as the captain expertly guides the craft through the current. There's usually a tugboat or smaller vessel making its way on the river as well, providing additional scenic views. Look for the giant pelicans that call the dock their home, but be careful: you don't want to find yourself underneath them if they are flying above!

4610 Ocean St., Atlantic Beach, FL 32233
(904) 241-9969
stjohnsriverferry.com

TIP
Prices and times for the ferry can be found online. Tickets can easily be purchased with credit and debit cards.

TAKE A WALK ON THE WILD SIDE
AT THE JACKSONVILLE ZOO AND GARDENS

Named one of the top 25 zoos in the country, the Jacksonville Zoo just keeps racking up the awards! Innovative habitats, an interactive children's play area, and stunning botanical gardens are just some of the reasons why visitors flock to the zoo. Noteworthy exhibits include a Manatee Critical Care Center, a new *African Forest* exhibit, and the highly praised *Land of the Tiger*. Also of special interest is the *Stingray Bay* touch tank and the ever-popular Zoo Train, which winds throughout the park. On a hot day, grab a snow cone, or frolic around on the splash pad to cool off before escaping to the *Range of the Jaguar*, where you'll find both big cats and tiny forest creatures. The Jacksonville Zoo has something to offer year-round for young and old alike. With over 2,000 species of rare and exotic animals and a firm commitment to improve and innovate, the Jacksonville Zoo is sure to make your visit a memorable one.

370 Zoo Parkway
(904) 757-4463
www.jacksonvillezoo.org

TIP

Feel free to pack a cooler and enjoy a picnic on the grounds; outside food and drink are permitted.

LEARN FROM THE PAST
AT THE KINGSLEY PLANTATION

Providing valuable insight into the lives of landowners and slaves in the 19th century, the Kingsley Plantation paints a vivid picture of these challenging times. What makes this particular plantation unique is not that it housed extensive orange groves and timberland but that the wife of the owner was a freed slave herself. Anta Majigeen Ndiaye (Anna) Kingsley was purchased by Zephaniah and later freed. During their time together at the Kingsley Plantation, Anna helped to run and manage its daily operations. Today, the estate stands as a window into a chapter of history that shaped our nation and continues to echo in our culture today. Take a tour of the grounds, and see the main house, kitchen house, barn, and remnants of the original tabby (an early form of cement crafted with sand, water, and crushed oyster shells) slave quarters.

11676 Palmetto Ave.
(904) 641-7155
www.nps.gov

TRAVERSE THE CURRENTS OF TIME
AT THE MUSEUM OF SCIENCE AND HISTORY

As the city's most popular attraction of its kind, the Museum of Science and History is known for its stimulating exhibits and innovative methods of reaching out to the community. Located steps away from the iconic Friendship Fountain and looking out over stunning views of downtown Jacksonville and the St. Johns River, MOSH (as the locals call it) is a must-visit. Spend the afternoon browsing one of the temporary traveling exhibits or enjoying one of the permanent core displays such as *JEA Power Play*. Dedicated to regional history and the sciences, the *Currents of Time* permanent exhibit takes you through centuries of North Florida's backstory in a stunning visual display. The Hixon Native Plant Courtyard and the Florida Naturalist's Center will help you get in touch with the region's natural life, while the Bryan-Gooding Planetarium will take you soaring into space. There's always something new for the whole family when you visit MOSH, which is why visitors keep coming back again and again.

1025 Museum Cir.
(904) 396-6674
themosh.org

TUNE IN
TO THE JACKSONVILLE SYMPHONY

Founded in 1949, the Jacksonville Symphony is a cultural treasure the community is grateful to call its own. Recognized as a world-class institution, the Symphony has been honored over the airwaves, as well as at the nation's capital, and has hosted the likes of Pavarotti, Duke Ellington, and Audra McDonald (just to name a few). As one of the few symphonies graced with a dedicated concert hall, the Jacksonville Symphony enjoys incredible acoustics, a spacious musician's lounge, and instrument lockers at the Robert E. Jacoby Symphony Hall. Playing for nearly 255,000 people every year in over 300 performances, the Jacksonville Symphony doesn't limit its performances to concert halls alone; it also performs at venues throughout the community at a variety of events. It's easier than ever to experience the Jacksonville Symphony, and with shows framed around Star Wars, Nintendo, and Harry Potter, it's never been more fun!

300 Water St. #200
(904) 354-5547
www.jaxsymphony.org

TIP

The symphony is dedicated to educating children about and exposing them to classical music and even offers free and discounted youth tickets.

CELEBRATE AFRICAN AMERICAN HERITAGE
AT THE RITZ THEATRE AND MUSEUM

Located in what was known as the Harlem of the South during it's heyday between 1921 and the 1970s, the Ritz Theatre was rebuilt and reopened in 1999. Serving today as one part museum and one part theatre, it is considered a mecca for African American heritage in Florida. A visit to the Ritz Theatre is an invitation to observe and learn from the past while joining in today's conversations that bring awareness and change to modern-day culture. Enjoy a play, witness local talent, watch a dance troupe showcase their moves, and hear voices from the past come alive as you relive their story through performance art. The Ritz Theatre is located in the historic LaVilla neighborhood and is an important part of Jacksonville that everyone should get to know.

829 N. Davis St.
(904) 632-5555
www.ritzjacksonville.com

PICNIC
UNDER TREATY OAK

Jacksonville boasts the largest urban park system in the states with 114 square miles of preserved land. One of the smallest of the 400-plus city green spaces is Jessie Ball duPont Park, also known as Treaty Oak Park. At the center of the 7-acre park sits a 250-year-old live oak that makes a massive statement amid the urban landscape of apartments and skyrises. Possibly predating the founding of the city itself, Treaty Oak was rescued from destruction by the surrounding development thanks to the efforts of *Times Union* reporter Pat Moran and philanthropist and Garden Club member Mrs. Jessie duPont. The park exists on land formerly occupied by a popular amusement venue called Dixieland Park, which opened in 1907. Today, the Treaty Oak's huge branches spread approximately 190 feet in diameter, and the trunk itself measures 25 feet around! Experts agree it could live another 400 years. Treaty Oak Park is a peaceful oasis for the city and one it aims to protect for generations to come.

1123 Prudential Dr.
(904) 630-2489
www.coj.net

WATCH A HISTORICAL REENACTMENT
AT FORT CLINCH STATE PARK

Fourteen hundred acres of Florida's natural wild await you when you visit Fort Clinch State Park on Amelia Island. Named for the 19th-century Civil War-era fort that calls the park home, Fort Clinch is strategically located at the tip of the peninsula overlooking the Saint Marys River. Views of Cumberland Island, Georgia, can also be seen from the walls of the fort once inhabited by Union soldiers. The park enjoys campgrounds, miles of hiking trails, paved roads for biking under canopies of oaks, plenty of birdwatching, and sharks' teeth hunting. The best time to visit is the first weekend of every month when live soldier reenactments occur and the cannons are set off as part of the pageant of military maneuvers. Explore the fort's empty hallways, check out the bunkhouses, and get a glimpse into the kitchens and officers' rooms. It's sure to be a walk back in time you won't soon forget.

2601 Atlantic Ave., Fernandina Beach, FL 32034
(904) 277-7274
www.floridastateparks.org/fortclinch

PERUSE THE ART OF OUR TIME
AT THE MOCA

Celebrating the art, artists, and ideas of our time, the Museum of Contemporary Art Jacksonville houses an exemplary collection of colorful works and traveling exhibits displayed in a variety of mediums. Focusing on works crafted from 1960 to the present, MOCA (as it's referred to locally) was formed in 1927 as the Jacksonville Fine Arts Society and has undergone an evolution of change and enhancements over the years. Finding its permanent home in 1999 on Laura St., the museum consists of a 60,000-square-foot, 6-story building. In addition to an entire floor just for kids, the museum houses a theatre, a café, a museum shop, educational facilities, and plenty of space for both permanent collection displays and traveling exhibits. The museum's commitment to the community is obvious with public events, artist Q&As, summer art camps, and public outreach. A visit to MOCA promises to engage and inspire you as you witness the art of our time.

333 N. Laura St.
(904) 366-6911
mocajacksonville.unf.edu

CRUISE THROUGH
THE BRUMOS COLLECTION

Time travel back to the early days of automobile history when you visit the Brumos Collection, an exhibition dedicated to the development of automobiles through the practice of racing. The collection includes vehicles designed over the course of three centuries and tells the story of how each generation improved upon the previous one with breakthroughs in engineering by the builders of Indy-style race cars and modern Porsche racers, among others. Interactive displays bring those stories to life and showcase the passion and dedication it took to bring such innovation to the field of racing and eventually to the masses. Pay homage to this rare piece of history by discovering these stories and perusing this display of modern technology that is distinctly the Brumos Collection.

5159 San Pablo Rd S.
(904) 373-0375
thebrumoscollection.com

TIP
All tickets must be purchased online in advance. No tickets are sold at the door.

MEANDER THROUGH THE GARDENS
AT CUMMER MUSEUM OF ART AND GARDENS

A walk through the Cummer Museum of Art and Gardens feels personal, as if you could be touring someone's estate. In fact, the museum's original collection and gardens were the personal property of Ninah Cummer who, upon her death, bequeathed her collection to what is now the Cummer Museum. Today, the museum has been rebuilt and expanded to include more than 5,000 objets d'art in its permanent collection. Offering a diverse range of exhibits both permanent and traveling, the museum houses art from as far back as 2100 BC to contemporary pieces. One of the museum's prime treasures is it's three historic sunken gardens located on two-and-a-half acres of land along the St. Johns River. The Olmstead garden, the English Garden, and the Italian Garden are prime examples of horticulture and landscape design from the early 20th century that exist today to delight, educate, and inspire visitors to the Cummer.

829 Riverside Ave.
(904) 356-6857
www.cummermuseum.org

TAKE A SELFIE TOUR
OF THE JACKSONVILLE MURALS

As the largest city by far in Florida, there is a lot of uncovered building space for outdoor muralists to work their craft. While the Walls of Wynwood are famously situated in one popular district, Jacksonville's murals are spread far and wide throughout the individual neighborhoods that make up North Florida. From silos to warehouses, from restaurants to garages, no space seems off limits to the artist's imagination. In fact, there are over 100 murals spread throughout town. If you'd like to take a tour by foot, a great place to begin is Hemming Park, where you'll find at least five murals within eyeshot, in addition to other types of public art. You can find a full map of Jacksonville's murals and public art online, where you can explore the diverse range of colors, concepts, and public statements these murals are sometimes designed to make while plotting your course accordingly.

www.visitjacksonville.com

Photo courtesy of Amy West

SHOPPING AND FASHION

SHOP WITH
THE COOL KIDS
IN FIVE POINTS

Once a struggling alternative strip of shops, today the Five Points area in Riverside is fresh and fun. With a youthful creative crowd, hip restaurants, and boutiques full of fascinating finds, it's easy to spend the day here. A short distance from the Riverside Arts Market, the Cummer Museum, and Memorial Park, Five Points offers vintage fashion, wine, indie flicks, and rooftop bars. Walkable from both the Riverside neighborhoods and high-rise business offices, the crowd stays diverse while the shopping never ceases to satisfy and delight. There's always something new and creative for you to discover at Five Points.

Park St.

5pointsjax.com

SUPPORT LOCAL ARTISTS
AT ART WALK

On the first Wednesday of every month, rain or shine, the heart of downtown buzzes with a kaleidoscope of color, music, and creativity. An average estimate of 5,000 attendees make their way downtown to explore the work of more than 100 artists, vendors, performing artists, and musicians featured at downtown Jacksonville's Art Walk. With more than 35 venues playing host to the artists on display, it's a great way to discover businesses you've never stepped foot in before. Each month has a new theme based on holidays, local interests, or what's on trend. It's an engaging display of art and culture and an ideal destination for picking up a handcrafted gift while supporting local artists.

214 N. Hogan St. #120
(904) 634-0303
downtownjacksonville.org/first-wednesday-art-walk

COLLECT YOUR NEXT ART PIECE
AT ATLANTIC BEACH ARTS MARKET

Atlantic Beach Arts Market is an artists' co-op with 5,000 square feet of shared space used for classes, workspace, and retail. Discover treasures of all kinds from over 90 artists and vendors working in a plethora of mediums from canvas to clay. ABAM (as the locals call it) offers up wall art, jewelry, paintings, glass, and vintage finds for your decorating inspiration. If you can't find the artisanal item you're searching for, you can learn how to make it. Every month at ABAM, you can choose from a variety of classes like watercolor painting, acrylic pouring, wire wrapping, and more. All 5,000 square feet are climate controlled, so even on the hottest or rainiest Florida days, ABAM is your go-to place for handcrafted finds.

1805 Mayport Rd., Atlantic Beach, FL 32233
(904) 372-7442
atlanticbeachartsmarket.com

ENJOY THE BEACH LIFE
AT BEACHES TOWN CENTER

Just 12 miles from downtown Jacksonville, where Atlantic Boulevard meets the ocean, sits the Beaches Town Center. It's the destination with the most traffic at the Beaches because of the wealth of shopping, dining, lodging, entertainment, and recreation to be found there. Sip on gourmet coffee; jive on a late-night dance floor; luxuriate with a spa service; or have a one-of-a-kind sandwich, salad, or dessert. When you're not trying a new cocktail or getting footloose in a trendy venue, discover the unique offerings of local boutiques. Beach chic, boho, fine leather, and accessories are just the start of the treasure trove of items you'll find at the Beaches Town Center. Just a hop, skip, and a jump from the shore, it has everything you need within walking distance for the perfect day out.

200 1st St., Neptune Beach, FL 32266
(904) 241-1026
beachestowncenter.com

TIP
Download the Flowbird app for seamless parking.

LOSE YOURSELF
IN CHAMBLIN BOOKMINE

With nearly 60,000 square feet of space filled to the brim with every kind of book imaginable, Chamblin Bookmine is legendary on the First Coast. Offering not one but two locations, you can also explore Chamblin's Uptown in Jacksonville's core while sipping on a latte from the store's cafe. Chamblin's owners have plans to expand their already massive main location. Once complete, it may be safe to conclude that if your desired title isn't there, it may not exist. In an era ruled by online shopping, it's refreshing to stroll through a brick-and-mortar bookstore and let yourself be awed by the massive stacks of books surrounding you. Since 1976, Chamblin Bookmine has been the place to discover rare or hard-to-find titles, delve into works by local authors, or lose track of time as you wander the aisles.

4551 Roosevelt Blvd.
(904) 384-1685
www.chamblinbookmine.com

WANDER
THROUGH SAN MARCO

Jacksonville's historic San Marco isn't just a great place to shop trendy boutiques; it also boasts a thriving art and culinary scene. Three stately lions, symbols of the biblical St. Mark, stand watch over San Marco Square, paying homage to its namesake in Venice. Visitors can find craft cocktails, bath and body products, best-selling books, and home goods. See a show at Theatre Jacksonville, indulge in a delicious sweet treat at Amaretti Desserts, and see if you can find The Parlour—one of Jacksonville's few speakeasies (Hint: go to the Grape and Grain Exchange and think "library"). Walk along the historic neighborhood streets, and enjoy the romance offered by the stately oaks and timeless architecture. It's a neighborhood shopping center that offers all the charm and elegance of a European destination, right here in the center of the Bold New City of the South.

San Marco Blvd.
visitjacksonville.com/neighborhoods/san-marco

GO TREASURE HUNTING
AT RIVERSIDE ARTS MARKET

Locals agree that one of the best "go-to" destinations in Jax to score a First Coast handmade treasure or just to socialize with old and new friends alike is the Riverside Arts Market. Situated on the banks of the St. Johns River, the market's year-round shade helps visitors stay comfortable thanks to its location under the Fuller Warren Bridge. Little ones enjoy face painting, balloon artists, and sweet treats like the ever-present, fresh-made kettle corn while grown-ups stock up on local produce, shop for unique gifts, or nosh on wood-fired pizza at one of the ubiquitous food trucks. Dine *al fresco* in the market's amphitheater, and take in musical entertainment provided by the constant stream of local musicians performing center stage. Pet owners rejoice in how fur-friendly Riverside Market is. Often, you'll see furry friends in the Riverside Market area dressed up to compete in costume shows or pet parades. If you're looking for the "real" Jacksonville, you'll find it in the collective creations that make up the experience of Riverside Arts Market.

715 Riverside Ave.
(904) 389-2449
riversideavondale.org/ram-home

TIP

Make a day of it, and receive free admission
on the first weekend of every month at the Cummer
Museum of Art and Gardens right next door to
Riverside Arts Market.

UPDATE YOUR LOOK
AT SAWGRASS MARKETS

Conveniently located just outside of TPC, Sawgrass Markets are more than a neighborhood shopping center; they are a destination. Serving the Ponte Vedra Beach community and beyond, the markets recently underwent a major facelift, transforming it into a modern town square with walkable shopping and dining and easy access to galleries, salons, and a supermarket. Update your look at one of the fashion-forward boutiques such A'Propos Boutique, or score your next timeless piece of collectible home furnishings at J Turner and Company. Wrap up your shopping day with a glass of wine as you soak up the warmth of a clear Florida afternoon at the Italian restaurant Andiamo, and bask in the lifestyle that makes living here so special.

215 Tourside Dr., Ponte Vedra Beach, FL 32082
www.sawgrassvillagepvb.com

TRANSFORM OLD TO NEW
AT ECO RELICS

Salvaged building materials, 50,000 square feet of antiques, and custom craftsmanship await you at Eco Relics. Considered one of the largest antique stores in the region, Eco Relics exists to re-purpose once-discarded fixtures and home goods. Saving tons of still-usable materials from already packed landfills, Eco Relics stands behind its reuse/recycle philosophy. Whether you are looking for lumber with extra character, vintage hardware, rare antiques, or custom woodwork, you're sure to find a priceless treasure during a visit to Eco Relic's massive warehouse.

106 Stockton St.
(904) 330-0074
ecorelics.com

FALL IN LOVE
WITH HISTORIC FERNANDINA BEACH

Just 20 minutes from Jacksonville's International Airport, the Isle of Eight Flags, also known as Amelia Island, is a unique getaway for an afternoon of shopping. Boutiques, eateries, and novelty stores await you in Historic Fernandina Beach complemented by waterfront views of the beautiful Amelia River. Downtown Fernandina Beach is overflowing with character and charm. Fall in love with your new favorite art piece, enjoy a drink at Florida's oldest pre-Prohibition bar, or find that special piece of jewelry you have been looking for. Colorful murals make for great photo ops. When the sun gets warm, treat yourself to a scoop of ice cream. This National Historic District spans over 50 blocks and is rich in activities that will inspire you to return again and again.

102 Centre St., Amelia Island, FL 32034
(904) 277-0717
www.ameliaisland.com/Shopping

WALK AND SHOP
AT THE SHOPPES OF AVONDALE

As one of the oldest historic neighborhoods in Jacksonville, Avondale is characterized by stately architecture, romantic tree-lined streets, and a warm Southern sensibility. Spend an afternoon at the Shoppes of Avondale indulging in a slice of gourmet cake at Biscottis, then meander down the sidewalks in search of unique gift ideas or classic wardrobe staples at one of the many boutiques. The available dining has a diverse appeal with everything from Mediterranean fare and pizza to seafood and even a classic neighborhood diner. Shoppes range from art galleries to home design and ladies' and children's boutiques to fine jewelry. Enjoy the ease and charm of this walkable shopping center as you take in one of Jacksonville's iconic historic districts.

3620 St. Johns Ave.
(904) 388-2118
shoppesofavondale.com

SATISFY YOUR SWEET TOOTH
AT SWEET PETE'S CANDY

Aptly called the Sweetest Destination on Earth, Sweet Pete's Candy is truly the tastiest jewel in the heart of Jacksonville. After an appearance on the reality TV show *The Profit*, mom-and-pop business owners Pete and Allison Behringer transformed their historic home-based candy shop into a landmark downtown destination that's truly larger than life. Located in a stately historic building, Sweet Pete's is a colorful oasis bursting with imaginative concoctions. Bejeweled chandeliers hang from the ceiling while multicolored confections line the walls. Take a tour and see where the magic happens in Sweet Pete's candy factory, or step up your skill set and take a candy-making class. Then, stock up on flavorful sweet treats beloved by the young and old alike.

400 N Hogan St.
(904) 376-7161
www.sweetpetescandy.com

TIP

Make sure to accept your free sea salt caramel upon arrival; it's Sweet Pete's signature confection.

MAKE TIME FOR TEA
AT ASHES BOUTIQUE AND TEA ROOM

Ashes Boutique and Tea Room is a family-owned beachside destination that will quickly become a tradition for your family. Casually chic, this coastal boutique is the perfect place to shop for gift items for that special lady in your life. Blending art and fashion, owner Dana Roby transforms her custom charcoal drawings into timeless treasures by applying them to garments and home goods you'll only find at Ashes. Named after Dana's daughter, Ashes Boutique practically glows with shades of white, grey, and rose in the softest cotton fabrics complete with lacy details. Don't forget to make time for tea before or after you shop. Roby's homemade tea sandwiches and desserts will fill a special spot in your soul while the feminine details and elegant atmosphere lift your spirits. Be sure to make reservations for tea; available spots fill up quickly!

332 2nd St. S., Jacksonville Beach, FL 32250
(904) 270-0220
ashesboutique.com

TIP

Set aside some time to explore other shops on the street. Located in the middle of this charming seaside village, there are plenty of shabby chic home decor and antique shops you will also want to visit.

GET YOUR RETAIL THERAPY
AT ST. JOHNS TOWN CENTER

As the premier shopping destination in North Florida, the St. Johns Town Center is an all-in-one shopping, dining, and entertainment complex. With over 175 stores and more than 20 dining outlets, you might find it difficult to cover the entire center in one day. This open-air shopping destination houses everything from Target to Tiffany's and is conveniently located in the center of Jacksonville with easy access to the beaches and downtown. Find your way out of the Escape Game room, track down your new favorite outfit at Nordstrom, enjoy fresh fare at True Food Kitchen, or shop for home goods at Pottery Barn. If you're looking for retail therapy, the St. Johns Town Center has you covered.

4663 River City Dr.
(904) 998-7507
www.simon.com/mall/st-johns-town-center

Photo courtesy of becphotography

SUGGESTED ITINERARIES

DATE NIGHT

Wine and Dine at Eleven South Bistro & Bar, 2
Celebrate in Style at Cowford Chophouse, 27
Chat with the Chef at Restaurant Doro, 10
Walk and Shop at the Shoppes of Avondale, 125
Enjoy the Bird's-Eye View at River and Post's
    Rooftop Lounge, 12
Enjoy a Taste of France at Orsay, 22
Find Your Vintage at Royal Palms Village Wine & Tapas, 30
Reserve a Seat at Salt's Kitchen Table, 24

FAMILY DAY

Become a Sandcastle Artisan at Opening of the Beaches, 57
Have Good Old-Fashioned Fun with the Jacksonville Jumbo
    Shrimp, 78
Go Behind the Scenes at Sally Dark Rides, 58
Bike the Baldwin Rail Trail, 66
Attend a Night Feeding at Catty Shack Ranch, 92
Make a Splash at Adventure Landing, 62

Meander through the Gardens at Cummer Museum of Art and
    Gardens, 109
Take a Walk on the Wild Side at the Jacksonville Zoo and
    Gardens, 98

BEACH DAY

Look to the Skies at the Sea and Sky Air Show, 40
Go Tiki at Flask and Cannon, 13
Become a Sandcastle Artisan at Opening of the Beaches, 57
Stand-Up Paddleboard at Jax Surf and Paddle, 84
Hunt for Sharks' Teeth at Guana Reserve's Middle Beach, 68
Drive on the Beach at Huguenot Memorial Park, 70
Explore Skeleton Beach, 74
Enjoy the Beach Life at Beaches Town Center, 117

KICK IT WITH FRIENDS

Go Tiki at Flask and Cannon, 13
Think Small at Mini Bar Donuts, 21
Drink Your Trail Off on the Jacksonville Ale Trail, 16
Order Tapas on the Rooftop at the Casa Marina Hotel, 90
Feel the Island Vibes at Lemon Bar, 17
Have a Spa Day at the Ritz-Carlton, 83
Make Time for Tea at Ashes Boutique and Tea Room, 128
Get in the Spirit at Manifest Distillery, 18

A DAY WITH HISTORY

Learn from the Past at the Kingsley Plantation, 100

Walk through History at the Beaches Museum, 88

Walk and Shop at the Shoppes of Avondale, 125

Traverse the Currents of Time at the Museum of Science and
History, 101

Celebrate African American Heritage at the Ritz Theatre and
Museum, 104

Watch a Historical Reenactment at Fort Clinch State Park, 106

Cruise through the Brumos Collection, 108

A BREATH OF FRESH AIR

Make a Splash at Adventure Landing, 62

Picnic under Treaty Oak, 105

Go Camping at Kathryn Abbey Hanna Park, 69

Take a Walk on the Wild Side at the Jacksonville Zoo and
Gardens, 98

Get Your Retail Therapy at St. Johns Town Center, 130

Take a Hike at Fort Caroline National Memorial, 95

GET SPORTY

Beat Feet at the Gate River Run, 73

Play like a Champion at the Stadium Course, 67

Support Du-u-u-uval at a Jacksonville Jaguars Game, 75

Attend THE PLAYERS Championship, 80

• •

Tailgate before the Florida-Georgia Game, 45

Finish the Donna, 76

HIPSTER FUN

Watch a Silver Screen Classic at San Marco Theatre, 51

Lose Yourself in Chamblin Bookmine, 118

Listen Up at the Blue Jay Listening Room, 46

Go Treasure Hunting at Riverside Arts Market, 120

Take a Selfie Tour of the Jacksonville Murals, 110

Shop with the Cool Kids in Five Points, 114

Transform Old to New at Eco Relics, 123

Jam On at Porchfest, 50

ACTIVITIES BY SEASON

SPRING

Get Footloose at Dancin' in the Streets, 44

Traverse the Globe at the World of Nations Celebration, 55

Beat Feet at the Gate River Run, 73

Meander through the Gardens at Cummer Museum of Art and
    Gardens, 109

Become a Sandcastle Artisan at Opening of the Beaches, 57

Attend THE PLAYERS Championship, 80

Listen to Blues on the Beach at Springing the Blues, 52

Admire the Luxury at *Concours d'Elegance*, 91

Watch the Showdown Unfold at Fish to Fork, 56

SUMMER

Go Tiki at Flask and Cannon, 13

Take a Dip at Dreamette, 9

Celebrate Your Independence during 4th of July in
    Jax Beach, 38

Drive on the Beach at Huguenot Memorial Park, 70

Chill Out at the Jacksonville Jazz Festival, 43

Make a Splash at Adventure Landing, 62

Stand-Up Paddleboard at Jax Surf and Paddle, 84

• •

Have Good Old-Fashioned Fun with the Jacksonville Jumbo
    Shrimp, 78
Thrill to an Airboat Adventure on the St. Johns River, 63
Watch a Historical Reenactment at Fort Clinch State Park, 106

FALL

Embrace the Harvest at Congaree and Penn, 26
Start Thanksgiving at Pete's Bar, 49
Get Your Fill of Pumpkin Spice at Cinotti's Bakery and
    Sandwich Shop, 7
Look to the Skies at the Sea and Sky Air Show, 40
Tailgate before the Florida-Georgia Game, 45
Support Du-u-u-uval at a Jacksonville Jaguars Game, 75
Bike the Baldwin Rail Trail, 66

WINTER

Take a Walk on the Wild Side at the Jacksonville Zoo and
    Gardens, 98
Peruse the Art of Our Time at the MOCA, 107
Sip on a Cup of Joe at Bold Bean Coffee Roasters, 5
Go Camping at Kathryn Abbey Hanna Park, 69
Finish the Donna, 76
Make Time for Tea at Ashes Boutique and Tea Room, 128
Take a Hike at Fort Caroline National Memorial, 95
Cruise through the Brumos Collection, 108

• •

INDEX

26.2 with Donna, 76

4th of July in Jax Beach, 38, 137

Adventure Landing, 62, 133, 135, 137

Alhambra Dinner Theatre, 41

Angie's Subs, 19

Art Walk, 115

Ashes Boutique and Tea Room, 128, 134, 138

Atlantic Beach Arts Market, 116

Baldwin Rail Trail, 66, 133, 138

Beaches Museum, 88-89, 135

Beaches Town Center, 44, 117, 134

Bearded Pig, 34

Biscottis, 4, 125

Blue Jay Listening Room, 46, 136

Bold Bean Coffee Roasters, 5, 138

Brumos Collection, The, 108, 135, 138

Brunch at Vernon's, 6

Casa Marina Hotel, 90, 134

Catty Shack Ranch, 92, 133

Chamblin Bookmine, 118, 136

Cinotti's Bakery and Sandwich Shop, 7, 138

Clark's Fish Camp, 8

Concours d'Elegance, 91, 137

Congaree and Penn, 26, 138

CoRK Art District, 94

Cowford Chophouse, 27, 133

Cummer Museum of Art and Gardens, 109, 121, 137

Dancin' in the Streets, 44, 137

Downtown Fernandina Beach, 124

Dreamette, 9, 137

Eco Relics, 123, 136

Eleven South Bistro & Bar, 2, 133

Fish to Fork, 56, 137

Five Points, 53, 114, 136

Flask and Cannon, 13, 134, 137

Florida-Georgia Game Tailgating, 45, 135, 138

Florida Theatre, 48, 51

Fort Caroline National Memorial, 95, 135, 138

Fort Clinch State Park, 106, 135, 138

French Pantry, 14

Gate River Run, 73, 135, 137

Guana Reserve's Middle Beach, 68, 134

Huguenot Memorial Park, 70, 134, 137

Jacksonville Ale Trail, 16, 134

Jacksonville Arboretum & Gardens, 64-65

Jacksonville Beach Fishing Pier, 38, 79, 90

Jacksonville Equestrian Center, 72

Jacksonville Jaguars, 75, 82, 135, 138

Jacksonville Jazz Fest, 43, 137

Jacksonville Jumbo Shrimp, The, 78, 133, 138

Jacksonville Library Main Branch, 96

Jacksonville Murals, 110, 136

Jacksonville Porchfest, 50, 136

Jacksonville Symphony, 102

Jacksonville Zoo and Gardens, 98, 134-135, 138

Jax Surf and Paddle, 84

Kathryn Abbey Hanna Park, 69, 135, 138

Kingsley Plantation, 100, 134

Lemon Bar, 17, 134

M Shack, 20

Manifest Distillery, 18, 134

Maple Street Biscuit Company, 32

Mini Bar Donuts, 21, 134

Museum of Contemporary Art Jacksonville, 107

Museum of Science and History, 82, 101, 135

Opening of the Beaches, 57, 133-134, 137

Orsay, 22, 133

Pete's Bar, 49, 138

Restaurant Doro, 10

Ritz-Carlton, Amelia Island Spa, 83

Ritz Theatre and Museum, 104, 135

River and Post, 12, 133

Riverside Arts Market, 114, 120, 136

Royal Palms Village Wine and Tapas, 30

Safe Harbor Seafood Restaurant, 23

Sally Dark Rides, 58, 133

Salt, 24, 133

San Marco, 5, 29, 33, 51, 54, 119, 136

San Marco Theatre, 51, 136

Sawgrass Markets, 122

Sea and Sky Air Show, 40, 134, 138

Sea Serpent Tours, 63

Shoppes of Avondale, The, 4, 125, 133, 135

Skeleton Beach, 74, 134

Springing the Blues, 52, 137

St. Johns River Ferry, 74, 97

St. Johns River Taxi and Tours, 82

St. Johns Town Center, 130, 135

Stadium Course, The, 67, 80, 135

Sun Ray Cinema, 53

Sweet Pete's Candy, 126

TacoLu, 28

Taverna, 29

THE PLAYERS Championship, 80, 135, 137

Theatre Jacksonville, 54, 119

Town Hall, 33

Treaty Oak, 105, 135

V Pizza, 3, 13

Veterans Memorial Arena, 42

World of Nations, 55, 137